JOURNAL · OF MORAL THEOLOGY

VOLUME 14, ISSUE 1
JANUARY 2025

TOUCHING THE WOUNDS

EDITED BY
M. THERESE LYSAUGHT

JOURNAL · OF
M · O · R · A · L
THEOLOGY

Journal of Moral Theology is published semiannually, with regular issues in January and July. Our mission is to publish scholarly articles in the field of Catholic moral theology, as well as theological treatments of related topics in philosophy, economics, political philosophy, and psychology.

Articles published in the *Journal of Moral Theology* undergo at least two double blind peer reviews. To submit an article for the journal, please visit the "For Authors" page on our website at jmt.scholasticahq.com/for-authors.

Journal of Moral Theology is available full text in the *ATLA Religion Database with ATLASerials®* (RDB®), a product of the American Theological Library Association.
Email: atla@atla.com, www.atla.com.
ISSN 2166-2851 (print)
ISSN 2166-2118 (online)

Journal of Moral Theology is published by The Journal of Moral Theology, Inc.

Copyright © 2025 individual authors and The Journal of Moral Theology, Inc. All rights reserved.
Pickwick Publications, An Imprint of Wipf and Stock Publishers, 199 W. 8th Ave., Suite 3, Eugene, OR 97401
www.wipfandstock.com. ISBN: 979-8-3852-4294-8

JOURNAL · OF M·O·R·A·L THEOLOGY

EDITOR EMERITUS
Jason King, *St. Mary's University, San Antonio, TX*

EDITOR
M. Therese Lysaught, *Loyola University Chicago Stritch School of Medicine*

SENIOR EDITOR
William J. Collinge, *Mount St. Mary's University*

ASSOCIATE EDITORS
Mari Rapela Heidt, *Notre Dame of Maryland University*
Alexandre A. Martins, *Marquette University*
Mary M. Doyle Roche, *College of the Holy Cross*
Matthew Shadle, *Window Light*
Kate Ward, *Marquette University*

MANAGING EDITOR
Jean-Pierre Fortin, *St. Michael's College, University of Toronto*

EDITORIAL ASSISANT
Aaron Weisel, *Ave Maria University*

EDITORIAL BOARD
Christina Astorga, *University of Portland*
Jana M. Bennett, *University of Dayton*
James Caccamo, *St. Joseph's University*
Victor Carmona, *University of San Diego*
Carolyn A. Chau, *King's University College at Western University, Ontario*
Stan Chu Ilo, *DePaul University*
Meghan Clark, *St. John's University*
Dana Dillon, *Providence College*
Jorge Jose Ferrer, SJ, *Pontifical Catholic University of Puerto Rico*
Daniel Fleming, *St. Vincent's Health Australia/University of Notre Dame Australia*
Julia A. Fleming, *Creighton University*
Joseph Flipper, *University of Dayton*
Nichole M. Flores, *University of Virginia*
Craig A. Ford, Jr., *St. Norbert College*
Matthew J. Gaudet, *Santa Clara University*
Leo Guardado, *Fordham University*
Andrew Kim, *Marquette University*
Cory Labrecque, *Université Laval*
Amy Levad, *University of St. Thomas, MN*
Leocadie Lushombo, *Santa Clara University*
Christina G. McRorie, *Boston College*
Cory D. Mitchell, *PeaceHealth*
Suzanne Mulligan, *Institute for Social Concerns, University of Notre Dame*
Sheryl Overmyer, *DePaul University*
Anna Perkins, *University of the West Indies/St. Michael's Theological College, Jamaica*
Bernard G. Prusak, *John Carroll University*
Emily Reimer-Barry, *University of San Diego*
Alessandro Rovati, *Belmont Abbey College*
Tobias Winright, *St. Patrick's Pontifical University, Ireland*

Journal of Moral Theology
Volume 14, Issue 1
January 2025

Contents

Introduction: Touching the Wounds
   M. Therese Lysaught 1

Original Articles

Nebulous Populism and the Constellation of Agencies within the Philippine Catholic Church
   Edryan Paul J. Colmenares 5

Reimagining Catholic Peacebuilding Through Pope Francis's "Culture of Encounter": The Case of Nigeria's Niger Delta Region
   Martin Owhorchukwu Ejiowhor 24

Jessica Coblentz's *Dust in the Blood: A Theology of Life with Depression*: A Roundtable

Theologizing Across Psychology: Experiences of Depression, Trauma, and Moral Injury
   Stephanie C. Edwards and Catherine Yanko 57

Investigating Moral Injury: Thinking Beyond the Law-Conscience Binary
   Catherine Yanko 59

Christian Ethics, Trauma, and *Dust in the Blood*: Moving Toward Enfleshed Counter-Memory
   Stephanie C. Edwards 74

How (Not) to Theologize Psychological Distress: Lessons from Thinking Across Conditions
   Jessica Coblentz 89

BOOK REVIEWS

Roger Bergman, *Catholic Social Learning: Educating the Faith That Does Justice*
    Jens Mueller 108

Luke Bretherton, *A Primer in Christian Ethics: Christ and the Struggle to Live Well*
    Andrew Blosser 109

Lucas Briola, *The Eucharistic Vision of* Laudato Si': *Praise, Conversion, and Integral Ecology*
    Patrick Nolin 111

D. Glenn Butner, Jr., *Jesus the Refugee: Ancient Injustice and Modern Solidarity*
    Thomas Massaro 113

William T. Cavanaugh, Carlos Mendoza-Álvarez, OP, Ikenna Ugochukwu Okafor, and Daniel Franklin E. Pilario, eds., *Fratelli Tutti: A Global Commentary*
    Thomas Massaro 114

Geoffrey D. Claussen, Alexander Green, and Alan L. Mittelman, eds., *Jewish Virtue Ethics*
    Michael Vanzandt Collins 116

David Carroll Cochran, *The Catholic Case Against War: A Brief Guide*
    Marc Tumeinski 118

Holly Taylor Coolman, *Parenting: The Complex and Beautiful Vocation of Raising Children*
    Maria C. Morrow 120

Andrew Gustafson and Celeste Harvey, eds., *Finding Faith in Business: An Economy of Communion Vision*
    Bernard G. Prusak 122

Christopher J. Kellerman, *All Oppression Shall Cease: A History of Slavery, Abolitionism, and the Catholic Church*
    Anna Kasafi Perkins 124

David Chiwon Kwon, *Justice After War:* Jus Post Bellum *in the 21ˢᵗ Century*
    Nicholas Hayes-Mota 126

Léocadie W. Lushombo, *A Christian and African Ethic of Women's Political Participation: Living as Risen Beings*
    David Kwon.. 128

Robert McNamara. *The Personalism of Edith Stein: A Synthesis of Thomism and Phenomenology*
    Catherine Moon.. 130

Joseph Ogbonnaya, ed., *Perspectives on Psychic Conversion*
    Steven Umbrello 132

Bharat Ranganathan, *On Helping One's Neighbor: Severe Poverty and the Religious Ethics of Obligation*
    Ngoc Nguyen 134

Antonio D. Sison, ed., *Deep Inculturation: Global Voices on Christian Faith and Indigenous Genius*
    Joe Evans... 136

Andrew M. Yuengert, *Catholic Social Teaching in Practice: Exploring Practical Wisdom and the Virtues*
    Ferdinand Tablan... 138

Introduction: Touching the Wounds

M. Therese Lysaught

The painful wounds of the world are Christ's wounds. If we ignore pain, poverty, and suffering in our world, if we turn a blind eye to them out of indifference or cowardice, if we are unwilling to acknowledge the injuries we inflict (including the injuries inflicted in our churches), and conceal them from others . . . then we have no right to say to Christ, like Thomas the apostle when he touched Jesus's wounds: "My Lord and my God."

In the Gospels, the resurrected Jesus identifies himself with his wounds. They are proof of his identity. The wounded Christ is the real, living Christ. He shows us his wounds and gives us the courage not to conceal our own. . . . And whoever, like "doubting Thomas," gazes from the gloom of doubts at the wounds on the body of our world and in the hearts of our neighbors—precisely through that wounded humanity, through that image of the humanity that the Son of God took upon himself—see God. "I and the Father are one," said the one who bore our wounds.[1]

So writes the Czech priest, sociologist, philosopher, and theologian Tomáš Halík, in his powerful Lenten meditation *Touch the Wounds: On Suffering, Trust, and Transformation*. Halík unfolds the thickly recursive interplay between Christ's embodied wounds as the *sine qua non* theological hermeneutic and the wounds of the world as a privileged Christological locus. His evocative work echoes and intertwines two recent moments in Pope Francis's emerging vision for theology: *Ad Theologiam Promovendam*'s call for a "paradigm shift" for theology that "commits it, first of all, to being a *fundamentally contextual theology*"; and the encyclical *Dilexit Nos*, his compelling meditation on the mystery of the sacred heart.[2] Here,

---

[1] Tomáš Halík, *Touch the Wounds: On Suffering, Trust, and Transformation*, trans. Gerald Turner (University of Notre Dame Press, 2023), xi–xii.
[2] Pope Francis, *Ad Theologiam Promovendam* (November 1, 2023), no. 4 (emphasis in original; Italian text, original translation); and Pope Francis, *Dilexit Nos* (October 2024), www.vatican.va/content/francesco/en/encyclicals/documents/20241024-enciclica-dilexit-nos.html. For further discussion of Pope Francis's vision for theology, see M. Therese Lysaught, "Ad (Synodalem) Theologiam (Moralem) Promovendam," *Journal of Moral Theology* 13, no. 1 (2024): 5–11, doi.org/10.55476/001c.92079.

as for Halik (as well as for the late Gustavo Gutierrez and others before them), it is in Christ's wounds—his pierced heart—where God bridges the distance between God and humanity and we fully encounter the fire of God's unfathomable love. This wounded Christ is equally encountered where people are caught in the broken places of the world: "I never tire of repeating that Jesus told us this in the clearest terms possible: 'Just as you did it to one of the least of these my brethren, you did it to me' (Matthew 25:40). He now asks you to meet him there, in every one of our brothers and sisters, and especially in the poor, the despised and the abandoned members of society. What a beautiful encounter that can be!" (*Dilexit Nos*, no. 213).

This paradigm shift toward the wounds of the world as a privileged *locus theologicus* reverberates throughout this issue of the *Journal of Moral Theology*. Each essay takes as its starting point for analysis and theological development the particularities of different wounds that are simultaneously social, bodily, and ecclesial. From the wounds of depression, moral injury, and trauma, to populist scapegoating in the Philippines and violence in the Niger Delta region of Nigeria, each essay first touches a place of woundedness, interrogates the church and received theology, and from there points in new directions for both moral theology and ecclesial practice.

The focal point of this issue is Jessica Coblentz's generative monograph *Dust in the Blood: A Theology of Life with Depression*.[3] Coblentz, exemplifying the courage not to conceal her own wounds, provides one of the few critical and constructive theological engagements with the experience and realities of depression. In doing so, she offers a lens for exploring additional psycho-social wounds. This lens is taken up by Catherine Yanko and Stephanie Edwards in the roundtable on her book featured in this issue. In "Investigating Moral Injury: Thinking Beyond the Law-Conscience Binary," Yanko extends Coblentz's narrative and phenomenological framework to the experience of moral injury, deriving important critiques of the facile, abstract, two-dimensional notion of conscience rife in contemporary Catholic moral theology. In "Christian Ethics, Trauma, and *Dust in the Blood*: Moving Toward Enfleshed Counter-Memory," Edwards turns the lens to trauma. Drawing on fifteen years of ministering as a social worker directly serving "adults in various marginalized positions, chiefly the unhoused, refugees and immigrants, woman-identified survivors of violence, and all the intersections therein," she draws on Coblentz to begin to reimagine a Christian social ethic as "enfleshed counter-memory."

---

[3] Jessica Coblentz, *Dust in the Blood: A Theology of Life with Depression* (Liturgical Press Academic, 2022). See also Andrew Staron's review of *Dust in the Blood* in *Journal of Moral Theology* 12, no. 1 (2023): 150–151, doi.org/10.55476/001c.66258.

Coblentz responds to Yanko and Edwards, as well as wider critical engagement with her book, to extend her own analysis in "How (Not) to Theologize Psychological Distress: Lessons from Thinking Across Conditions." Among her key points, she notes how forms of "psychological" distress are often mistakenly localized to an individual's mind, interiorized to individual biology. She rightly counters that such conditions equally have social and political dimensions. Via these social wounds Coblentz, like Yanko, challenges the often oversimplified moral and theological categories that do further epistemological and moral violence to those who suffer.

That psychological distress cannot be siloed from politics comes to the fore in Edryan Paul J. Colmenares's article, "Nebulous Populism and the Constellation of Agencies within the Philippine Catholic Church." Colmenares's analysis could not be more timely for US readers. While particularities of the Philippines make clear that each context has its own local history and complicated landscape, studying the dynamics of populism fueled by scapegoating violence in one specific context may illuminate the way it works in others. Nonetheless, mapping the multifaceted ways in which the Filipino Catholic Church has interfaced with local populist movements, particularly under the Duterte regime, promises to be helpful not only to the Filipino church; it also provides a framework for exploring parallel dynamics in the US. At minimum, to extend Colmenares's conclusion, in both contexts "the elites within the Catholic Church [must] grow in recognition of the disenfranchised masses within their own nation and church community." They must, in Halík's words, touch the wounds in new ways.

Such a vision of recognition and connection is captured in Pope Francis's vision of the "culture of encounter." This hallmark of Francis's papacy forms the centerpiece of Martin Owhorchukwu Ejiowhor's "Reimagining Catholic Peacebuilding Through Pope Francis's 'Culture of Encounter': The Case of Nigeria's Niger Delta Region." Ejiowhor's starting point is the socio-politico-economic wound of natural resource-based violence that has plagued Nigeria's Niger Delta region for the past twenty years (with, of course, much longer tendrils of historic violence as well as psychological sequelae). Like Colmenares, Ejiowhor traces the multiple ways the Nigerian Catholic Church has interfaced with this violence and its surrounding politics, posing Francis's culture of encounter as the basis for ecclesial conversion. As he notes, a "reinvigorated ecclesial self-identity and prophetic witness, essential for the church's active contribution to global conflict transformation and sustainable social peace," is constitutive of the evangelizing mission of the church.[4]

The authors in this issue do not ignore the pain, poverty, and suffering in our world. They know that these are wounds of the resurrected Christ. As such, Halík challenges us:

> Resurrection is not "resuscitation," the return to a previous state. The Gospels tell us that Jesus was transformed beyond recognition by his experience of death. Not even his nearest and dearest could recognize him at first. He had to prove his identity by his wounds. In this book, I confess that I am incapable of believing in a God without wounds, a church without wounds, or a faith without wounds. Our faith too is constantly wounded by what we experience—in the world and in the church itself. But aren't its wounds—maybe more than a lot of things—a sign of its authenticity? Can a faith that bears no stigmata, a faith that cautiously avoids the Golgothas of our time, help to heal a wounded world?[5]

I do not doubt that as theology continues to touch the wounds of the world, it will be transformed beyond what we currently recognize as theology. I am equally convinced that only such a theology—bearing the stigmata—will actually help to heal the wounded places of the world and those inhabiting them.

---

[4] Martin Owhorchukwu Ejiowhor, "Reimagining Catholic Peacebuilding Through Pope Francis's 'Culture of Encounter': The Case of Nigeria's Niger Delta Region," *Journal of Moral Theology* 14, no. 1 (2025): 24.
[5] Halík, *Touching the Wounds*, xvii.

Nebulous Populism and the Constellation of Agencies within the Philippine Catholic Church

Edryan Paul J. Colmenares

Abstract: Many scholars who have studied populism consider it a nebulous concept, given the variety of causes that explain its formation. Some view it as emerging from failed liberal democracies with worsening economic inequalities. Others have viewed political disenfranchisement as a leading factor, while a handful relate it to socio-cultural and psychological yearnings for the kind of leader the populist leader embodies. This article explores how the emergence of Duterte's brand of populism in the Philippines may be understood, considering its history of attempting to establish a liberal democracy. Given that the Philippines is a predominantly Catholic nation, the author also locates the Catholic Church, its hierarchy, and members as a conglomerate of various agents within the populist movement. Lastly, the author explores how populism in the Philippines challenges the church's desire to be a church for and of the poor.

SCHOLARS WHO HAVE STUDIED POPULISM HAVE REVEALED that while it has a thin political ideology, several characteristics can help define and identify whether a government or movement is becoming populist. Some view it as emerging from failed liberal democracies with worsening economic inequalities. Others have viewed political disenfranchisement as a leading factor, while a handful relate it to socio-cultural and psychological yearnings for the kind of leader the populist leader embodies.[1] Other scholars relate it to the rise of social media and the absence of traditional gatekeeping agents in exchanging information on the Internet.[2] International Affairs expert Cas Mudde observed that

> [Populism] is growing in developing democracies in other parts of the world, most notably in Southeast Asia, the Middle East, and sub-Saharan Africa. . . . Given the even larger economic, social, and

---

[1] See Noam Gidron and Bart Bonikowski, "Varieties of Populism: Literature Review and Research Agenda," SSRN Scholarly Paper (Rochester, NY, 2013), doi.org/10.2139/ssrn.2459387.
[2] Agnes M. Brazal, *A Theology of Southeast Asia: Liberation-Postcolonial Ethics in the Philippines*, Duffy Lectures in Global Christianity (Maryknoll, NY: Orbis Books, 2019).

political diversity of these regions, it is harder to distinguish clear trends, although certain shared characteristics of populist actors can be determined.[3]

Given these factors, it is helpful to hold all these together and identify which factor has greater weight or influence in understanding the emergence of populism in particular contexts. In this article, I will explore how populism has emerged in the Philippines, making it possible for Rodrigo Duterte to be the preferred leader.

Then, using a typology of populist agents presented by James Keenan, I will explore the agency of the masses, the leader, and the opposition within the Catholic Church in the Philippines. Lastly, I will unpack how populism presents challenges and invitations to the Catholic Church's self-understanding and mission in the Philippines by considering the works of Fr. Flavie Villanueva and the role of the mission stations in the Diocese of Kalookan led by Bishop Pablo Virgilio "Ambo" David. I argue that understanding populism as emerging from the antagonistic relationship between two groups, especially in the Philippines, calls the elites within the Filipino Catholic Church to grow in recognition of the disenfranchised masses within their own nation and church community.

UNPACKING DUTERTE'S POPULISM: FRUSTRATIONS, ANXIETIES, AND HOPES OF THE FILIPINO

Despite the fact that "populism is a nebulous concept," sociologists Adele Webb and Nicole Curato assert that Rodrigo Duterte is a populist. Duterte manifests core characteristics from varying studies on populism. Without conflating nationalism and populism, Webb and Curato recognize that the Philippines is characterized by a populist nationalism they describe in this manner:

> Rather than tapping into issues of ethno-cultural identity, this type of populism mobilizes incendiary ideas of power, status, and hierarchy and takes the form of demands for national self-determination and struggles for national autonomy. The populist down/up antagonism (rather than in/out) structures political demands. The nation in its entirety becomes the underdog (down), pitted against an "elite" (up) who may be national or international and who are deemed illegitimate for being opposed to the nation's interests.[4]

---

[3] Cas Mudde and Cristóbal Rovira Kaltwasser, *Populism: A Very Short Introduction* (New York: Oxford University Press, 2017), 38.
[4] Adele Webb and Nicole Curato, "Populism in the Philippines," in *Populism Around the World* (Cham: Springer International, 2018), 50–52, doi.org/10.1007/978-3-319-96758-5_4.

This definition of populist nationalism provides a succinct description of the populism Duterte wields. He used "power, status, and hierarchy" to launch his political agenda as one who would fight the elites on behalf of his underdog supporters and meet their demands. One antagonism Duterte surfaces is resentment from the glaring socioeconomic inequality in the Philippines due to the neglect by longstanding political elites.

Ronald Mendoza and Leonardo Jaminola observed that various causes explain the growing Filipino preference for populist leaders. One factor is the inability of previous and incumbent political players to narrow the inequality gap in the Philippines, despite the constant economic growth the country has enjoyed in recent decades. The inequality gap is more pronounced in urban areas, where one sees the development of gated subdivisions and the rise of luxury condominiums beside swaths of increasingly congested urban settlements. Such "in-your-face inequality" has generated growing pressure for a pushback. They also noted that the "growing concerns over the challenges and risks associated with rapid urbanization—including the threat of crime and illegal drugs, rising transport costs and traffic, as well as economic uncertainty" are contributing factors favoring the populist Duterte.[5]

In another work, Nicole Curato observed that Duterte presents a dichotomy "between virtuous citizens versus hardened criminals"[6] involved in the illegal drug trade. By declaring during his campaign that there is a crisis caused by the pervasive problem of illegal drugs throughout the country, Duterte managed to tap into a "latent anxiety already existing in the public sphere."[7] In recent years, some communities have noted how the spread and use of illegal drugs has become a more noticeable and disturbing problem. Curato noticed how community leaders she interviewed felt that "they have been left to deal with this issue by themselves."[8] She notes from her field observations that the problem of illegal drugs has always been there. Communities bear the negative consequences of disrupted social relations caused by users and peddlers of illegal drugs. Yet, only Duterte brought this issue to the fore of national politics by making it a concern for the whole country. In doing so, he earned the image of someone who cared about the problems of people on the ground, and

---

[5] Ronald U. Mendoza and Leonardo M. Jaminola, "Is Duterte a Populist? Rhetoric vs. Reality," CIRSD, *Horizons: The Journal of International Relations and Sustainable Development* 15 (Winter 2020): 267–268.
[6] Nicole Curato, "Politics of Anxiety, Politics of Hope: Penal Populism and Duterte's Rise to Power," *Journal of Current Southeast Asian Affairs* 35, no. 3 (December 1, 2016): 94, doi.org/10.1177/186810341603500305.
[7] Curato, "Politics of Anxiety, Politics of Hope," 98.
[8] Curato, "Politics of Anxiety, Politics of Hope," 99.

promised he was willing to solve the problem by every means possible if and when he was elected president.

By surfacing this problem, Duterte implied that some people in government have turned a blind eye and should be held accountable. He tapped into the frustration and resentment felt by people whose concern about illegal drug use had gone unrecognized by previous administrations. In Duterte, Curato observed that "citizens who often find themselves hassled by petty thieves and addicts envision a sense of finality . . . even if it happens at the expense of due process. After all, what use is due process if it entails taking part in the slow and inefficient process of the criminal justice system?"[9] In her work with Webb, Curato notes how these manifested the failure of the liberal democracy project in the Philippines. Thus, in supporting Duterte and rejecting the groups advocating for liberal democracy, Duterte's supporters agree with his understanding of the crisis besieging the Philippines.[10]

The frustration and resentment that surfaced were not just directed toward an unresponsive government; it was also aimed at the political values and principles—human rights, due process, and so forth—that abated the pace of justice for citizens seeking a solution to the drug problem. Curato explains this by presenting Frederic Schaeffer's idea politics." "Privileged segments of society consider transparent and accountable governance as central to democratic practice, impoverished regarding how different socio-economic classes define "good communities view consideration and kindness as constitutive of 'good politics.'"[11] She asserts that this applies to Duterte's supporters, especially seeing that the latter have rejected the language and values used by the previous administration, which privileged decency over vulgarity, the clean over the corrupt, and rights over lives, especially since those values did not seem to motivate then incumbent officials in solving their woes. In her study with Webb, they observed that

> Duterte framed his attack by building on the antagonism between, on one hand, weak liberal institutions, the oligarchs that benefit from the system, and liberal signifiers such as human rights and, on the other hand, the interests of the nation and the popular sovereignty of the "people."[12]

In laying this bare, Duterte exposed the flaws of the system and identified antagonists to the people's progress. In cementing the mistrust people had with systems, processes, rule of law, human rights,

---

[9] Curato, "Politics of Anxiety, Politics of Hope," 100–101.
[10] Webb and Curato, "Populism in the Philippines," 60.
[11] Curato, "Politics of Anxiety, Politics of Hope," 96–97.
[12] Webb and Curato, "Populism in the Philippines," 60.

and incumbent politicians, he galvanized his image of an outsider to national politics willing to lead a government that "delivers because not despite of cutting corners."[13] Thus, those who would later criticize Duterte for his refusal to observe the rule of law and uphold human rights, especially during his anti-drug campaign, would be labeled "enemies of the people."

The frustration and resentment Duterte taps into have long been present, especially among the masses. One of the key arguments in Richard Heydarian's account of Duterte's ascension to the presidency is the "simmering public dissatisfaction with the post-Marcos 'elite democracy,' which failed to live up to its initial promise of social justice and sustainable development."[14] It is ironic that Duterte's election happened exactly three decades after Marcos, Sr.'s ouster during the EDSA Revolution, and that his presidency is sandwiched between Benigno Aquino III's and Ferdinand Marcos, Jr.'s. The former is the son of Corazon Aquino, whom the Filipinos elected as president to replace the dictator Marcos, Sr., who happens to be the latter's father.

Throughout the presidency of Duterte's predecessor Benigno Aquino III, the Philippines enjoyed an average GDP growth rate of 6.2% while significantly reducing unemployment and underemployment. When he finished his term, the World Bank changed their moniker for the Philippines from the "sick man of East Asia" to "the rising tiger,"[15] yet the masses barely felt this change. This just widened the existing income gap. "The rich had tripled their incomes from P630 billion in 2010 to P2.2 trillion in 2015—a 250 percent increase—as they consolidated or expanded their control of the banking, telecommunications, and property development sectors."[16] By 2016, fourteen Filipinos managed to land on the Billionaires List of *Forbes* but when Aquino started his presidency in 2010, there were only three Filipinos on the list. While this exclusive group of billionaires accounted for 11.3% of the country's GDP in 2016, the contribution of the bottom 20% did not reach 5%.[17]

While the previous argument focuses on economic disenfranchisement, Abinales and Amoroso mention other factors as well.[18] Thus, the failure of the liberal democracy project to deliver reform and

---

[13] Webb and Curato, "Populism in the Philippines," 61.
[14] Richard Javad Heydarian, *The Rise of Duterte* (New York: Springer, 2017), 11.
[15] Patricio N. Abinales and Donna J. Amoroso, *State and Society in the Philippines*, 2nd ed. (Lanham, MD: Rowman & Littlefield, 2017), 321.
[16] Abinales and Amoroso, *State and Society in the Philippines*, 323.
[17] Abinales and Amoroso, *State and Society in the Philippines*, 321–323.
[18] Abinales and Amoroso, *State and Society in the Philippines*, 337. For a more in-depth historical treatment, one may consult their chapter analyzing the first year of Duterte's presidency.

prosperity after the ouster of the dictator Marcos thirty years ago can also be understood in other forms of marginalization. The issue is not just about trickling down economic gains, but also addressing the frustrations and insecurities of the middle class and Filipinos' ambivalent attitude toward liberal democracy's power to improve their daily realities.[19]

LOCATING THE CHURCH WITHIN PHILIPPINE POPULISM

How does this understanding of populism help us identify and characterize various agents of populism as located within the Philippine church? Sociological and documentary resources illuminate this question. Journalist Adam Willis claims that

> in the Philippines, the church has emerged as the most prominent voice of dissent against a drug war that has claimed, by some estimates, more than twenty thousand lives. It is also under perpetual assault from a president intent on contesting the very essence of Philippine Catholicism. Having framed his 2015 campaign as a referendum on the legitimacy of the church, Duterte has forced religious leaders to choose between coveted political capital and their moral mandates.[20]

While this statement may be true in some sense, as unpacked below, it betrays a monolithic understanding of the Catholic Church in the Philippines. To look at how the Catholic Church is embroiled in this drug war and the broader phenomenon of Duterte's populism requires a deeper analysis than what Willis presents. Given the diversity of actors and views within the Catholic Church, I will use James Keenan's enumeration of the agents of populism to identify the varied ways members of the Catholic Church acts as agents of populism. Keenan identifies five groups of agents within the populist movement. These are:

> The masses themselves, their leaders, the wealthy who fund the leaders, other institutional opportunists who capitalize on the inroads made by the populist movement, and finally the so-called elite: the government's lawmakers who have the opportunity to respond but do not yet recognize the validity of those populists' claims regarding their

---

[19] Webb and Curato, "Populism in the Philippines," 60.
[20] Adam Willis and Eloisa Lopez, "Church vs. State: Philippine President Rodrigo Duterte's Brutal but Popular War on Drugs Has Forced the Catholic Church to Ask Itself a Defining Question: What Is Its Responsibility under an Immoral Regime?," *Virginia Quarterly Review* 95, no. 2 (June 17, 2019): 42.

own non-recognition and resulting inequities and subsequent alienation.[21]

In the subsequent sections, I will explore, per Keenan's description, how church members are found among the populist masses and also in the elites. It will be helpful to add how members of the church are considered agents opposed to the populist regime without necessarily lumping them automatically with the rest of the elites.

The Church among Populist Masses

Considering that the Philippines is a predominantly Christian and Catholic country, one can locate the church among the supporters of Duterte. Jayeel Cornelio, a sociologist of religion, and Erron Medina, a graduate researcher from the University of the Philippines, have pointed out that some Christians support Duterte because they agree that the problem of illegal drugs is a scourge to the Philippines. Some of the supporters Cornelio and Medina interviewed would even go as far as saying that Duterte's presidency was a godsend.[22] While Cornelio and Medina's study primarily focused on Protestant communities, another study by Cornelio notes that there are also members and leaders of the Catholic Church in the Philippines who support Duterte.[23]

Per Cornelio and Medina's interviews, those who support the drug war do so because they believe that "a strong and decisive" campaign is necessary since, given their circumstances, "a direct relationship exists between substance abuse and criminality."[24] They consider drug users and peddlers to be people who deliberately engage in sinful actions. Thus, "God gave us [this] government . . . to protect the innocent and punish the guilty. They have swords and guns for a reason."[25] I will return to this perspective on drug users and pushers below.

In a previous study, Webb and Curato noted:

---

[21] James F. Keenan, "Restoring Social Trust: From Populism to Synodality," *Theological Studies* 84, no. 1 (March 1, 2023): 199.
[22] Jayeel Serrano Cornelio and Erron Medina, "Christianity and Duterte's War on Drugs in the Philippines," *Politics, Religion, & Ideology* 20, no. 2 (June 2019): 159, doi.org/10.1080/21567689.2019.1617135.
[23] Jayeel Cornelio and Gideon Lasco, "Morality Politics: Drug Use and the Catholic Church in the Philippines," *Open Theology* 6, no. 1 (2020): 327. See Paterno Esmaquel, "Why Filipinos Believe Duterte Was 'Appointed by God,'" News, *Rappler*, June 28, 2019, www.rappler.com/newsbreak/in-depth/234115-why-filipinos-believe-duterte-appointed-by-god/.
[24] Cornelio and Medina, "Christianity and Duterte's War on Drugs."
[25] Cornelio and Medina, "Christianity and Duterte's War on Drugs," 160.

We offered ethnographic evidence that demonstrates how "virtuous citizens" who claim to have done everything to earn a decent living feel disdain for "addicts on street corners"—"the dangerous other." The anxiety deepens when Filipinos who invested time and resources to "virtuous projects," like volunteering in local livelihood programs or the church, feel that the future of their children is put in jeopardy if they make friends or enemies with these addicts. For the longest time, these anxieties were latent. . . . The enemy in this narrative is within the nation—the dangerous drug pushers, as well as the greedy and tone-deaf elites of Imperial Manila, including the corrupt justice system and those who turn a blind eye to the drug scourge.[26]

Given these, Duterte supporters feel justified in their support for his anti-drug war, especially since he is the only president who managed to make the problem of illegal drugs a national issue. This became more evident in performance satisfaction surveys, where Duterte continued to enjoy record-high trust and satisfaction ratings despite the reports of thousands of casualties in the anti-drug war. Most of the respondents in these surveys were aware of the killings taking place under his administration.[27] Cornelio and Medina observed that "the argument is that people feel safer now, which is why they remain supportive of the War on Drugs. For many people, according to another study, the killings are acceptable because 'these are the people that made our miserable lives even more miserable.'"[28] It must be noted that the satisfaction and preference for Duterte goes beyond support for his anti-drug campaign. It also signals a deep-seated frustration and resentment against the government and other civil society groups advocating for liberal democratic ideals Filipinos fought for during the past three decades.

The Church among Elites

When the Catholic Bishops Conference of the Philippines synthesized the diocesan synodal reports in preparation for the first meeting of the Synod on Synodality held in October 2023, they published the national synodal report, which articulates the various sentiments of the clergy, religious, and laypeople shared during the nationwide local and diocesan synodal conversations. Given the high response and participation rate noted in the national synodal report, it would be safe to assume that what the report contains approximates the current state of the Philippine Catholic Church. The earlier sections of the document presented the people's perceptions and observations about the clergy. The report notes:

---

[26] Webb and Curato, "Populism in the Philippines," 59.
[27] Cornelio and Medina, "Christianity and Duterte's War on Drugs," 168.
[28] Cornelio and Medina, "Christianity and Duterte's War on Drugs."

> Many of the underprivileged and those who were marginalized in society felt that they were also left out in the church. As the church is seen to be for the rich, the economically poor as well as those who are deprived of social acceptance are being left out. Dioceses with Catholics as minorities felt however, that they can identify more closely with those who were marginalized and persecuted, and for this reason they embodied a church of the poor and those suffering from bombings, intimidations, and persecutions. . . . When the poor speak out or try to voice an opinion, they are simply ignored or set aside as unimportant. Many people feel that only the donors and benefactors (dubbed as the "owners of the church") have a voice or are entitled to speak out.[29]

In his analysis, Keenan locates religious, cultural, and social leaders as a fourth group of agents who "use the populist leader and the populist masses for their own gain."[30] Keenan's description of religious and cultural leaders applies more to other sects like the *Iglesia ni Kristo* or the community of Apollo Quiboloy, rather than the Catholic Church.[31] Given Duterte's tirades and the state of the Catholic Church in the Philippines, some members of the Catholic community, especially the hierarchy, can be identified with the elites in the way Keenan described them as agents. He writes that the elites

> are in part responsible for the original non-recognition of what later emerged as a populist movement. In this they are similar to the masses they ignore: they each consider themselves victims and acquit themselves of any moral wrongdoing. The elite have overlooked many in their maintenance of liberal democracies and kept them in place in the elite's evident hierarchies. But often their agency, their "causative" role in the development of the populist claims, goes unacknowledged.[32]

As seen with how the populist masses in the Philippines have been disenfranchised, the elites within the Catholic Church may, unknowingly, have contributed to this disenfranchisement, given how they have been associated with the oligarchs and their treatment of the poor and marginalized. Furthermore, some sectors in civil society "expressed their concrete needs and grievances and challenged the

---

[29] "Salubong—The Philippine Catholic Church Synodal Report—SYNOD 2021–2023 Philippines," Synod 21–24 Philippines, August 19, 2022, synodphilippines.com/salubong-the-philippine-catholic-church-synodal-report/.
[30] Keenan, "Restoring Social Trust," 122.
[31] It maybe a different matter, though, for other Christian denominations and independent churches. Keenan's conception of the role of religious leaders is helpful in understanding the role leaders of Megachurches play as they support Duterte's War on Drugs. See Jayeel Cornelio and Ia Marañon, "A 'Righteous Intervention': Megachurch Christianity and Duterte's War on Drugs in the Philippines," *International Journal of Asian Christianity* 2, no. 2 (October 2019): 211–230, doi.org/10.1163/25424246-00202005.
[32] Keenan, "Restoring Social Trust," 124.

church to fight with them and for them," given that there is an expectation that it is part of the church's mission. Some indigenous peoples even expressed how they "see themselves as 'objects of missionary help,' but they are neglected in the area of evangelization."[33] Why is this so? How come the leaders or elites of the local church are unable to recognize the plight of the poor within the church and act accordingly?

Filipino moral theologian Rolando Tuazon provides possible answers. First, he observes that the Catholic Church in the Philippines is preoccupied with internal institutional matters rather than living out a preferential option for the poor and marginalized. Given the Philippine context, Tuazon sees what Pope Francis noted, that "in some people, we see an ostentatious preoccupation for the liturgy, for doctrine, and for the church's prestige, but without any concern that the Gospel has a real impact on God's faithful people and the concrete needs of the present time."[34] As if affirming what respondents have shared during the synodal consultations, Tuazon goes on to point out how the local church lacks a united front in being in solidarity with the poor facing problems such as "agrarian reform, demolition of informal settlements, contractualization of labor, minimum wage, union organization, and strikes."[35] Such an assessment challenges the Philippine church with what the Second Plenary Council of the Philippines articulated as its mission to become a church of the poor and for the poor.[36]

The second reason Tuazon points out is that church communities and organizations tend to undermine the voice and agency of the poor and marginalized in their programs and in articulating their vision for a just society. They are often viewed as mere recipients of these programs or outreach communities by church communities. He notes that his respondents often perceive "people in the Church . . . to be the ones who teach, direct, and guide."[37] Such an answer already signals how the poor and marginalized do not see themselves as part of those who are in the church.

Tuazon's third reason complements his second. If the poor and marginalized do not see themselves as part of the church, then one is

---

[33] "Salubong—The Philippine Catholic Church Synodal Report."
[34] Pope Francis, *Evangelii Gaudium*, no. 95 in Rolando A. Tuazon, "Social Discernment from the Margins: A Reappropriation of CST in Light of the Philippines' 2022 Elections," *Journal of Catholic Social Thought* 20, no. 1 (March 20, 2023): 58, doi.org/10.5840/jcathsoc20232014.
[35] Tuazon, "Social Discernment from the Margins," 59.
[36] Catholic Bishops Conference of the Philippines, *Acts and Decrees of the Second Plenary Council of the Philippines* (Manila: Catholic Bishops' Conference of the Philippines, 1992), nos. 125–127.
[37] Tuazon, "Social Discernment from the Margins," 59.

forced to ask: who forms the church? Tuazon asserts that the church is identified more with the middle and upper classes. He even emphasizes how the middle class is seen as mission partners, and those in the lower socioeconomic classes are considered recipients or beneficiaries of the church's mission work.[38]

Another reason Tuazon provides is the preoccupation the church has with "personal morality and sexual ethics." This often obviates people from seeing how the ethical tradition of the Catholic Church can contribute to societal transformation. When considering the broader Catholic population in the Philippines, Catholic social teaching or CST is considered "the best-kept secret of the church." For him, this tradition has not yet been integrated well into the Filipino Catholic faith[39] on account of a merely conceptual understanding of "solidarity and a preferential option for the poor." Thus, he sees this as a failure of church leaders to help Christians understand and appreciate the social mission of the church deeply tied to the call to engage in integral evangelization. More than just having to produce and disseminate knowledge of CST, the call is to more authentic witnessing.[40] At the heart of it is the incapacity to be moved and recognize the scandalous poverty and destitution experienced by the poor.

The reasons provided by Tuazon make sense when considering the National Synodal Report released by the Catholic Bishops' Conference of the Philippines, explored earlier. When asked how people see themselves *vis-à-vis* the Catholic Church, a variety of responses came from those who participated in the synodal consultations; some were surprised to find out that church leaders were interested in listening to their concerns. In other cases, respondents identified the inability of the church to journey with them considering the ministerial practice of clergy. In this case, some pointed out how their pastors are barely immersed in their communities and caught up with vices. Underprivileged groups felt they were being "left out in the church." Interestingly, dioceses in regions where the Catholics are a minority population are more identified with the poor and marginalized rather than the affluent and elites in the area. Then, there are "those who were demoralized or felt excluded" who "have left the church and no longer find the need to be part of it," as a result of clerical sexual abuse, priests who eventually have children, or the indifference they feel towards the "pastoral statements and programs of the church."[41]

---

[38] Tuazon, "Social Discernment from the Margins," 61.
[39] Tuazon, "Social Discernment from the Margins," 62.
[40] Tuazon, "Social Discernment from the Margins," 63–64.
[41] "Salubong—The Philippine Catholic Church Synodal Report," 3–4.

At this point, we have seen how the local church in the Philippines, its leaders, and some of its members are associated with the elites and how this association makes them an alienated and antagonized group within Duterte's populist regime.

The Church within the Opposition

While we have seen how some members and leaders of the Catholic Church in the Philippines count among the elites who may have been oblivious to the lives and woes of the poor, that is not the case for the entire Catholic Church. If we could locate both masses and elites within the same ecclesial community, those who resist and oppose Duterte's populism could also be found within the same church. Locating the Catholic Church within the opposition and understanding their agency is also important since we risk undermining their efforts at resistance by simply lumping them together with the groups of agents identified by Keenan.

In the last chapter of their book, *State and Society in the Philippines*, Abinales and Amoroso give us a glimpse of the first year of Duterte's administration. They wrote:

> Once elected, Duterte gave the Philippine National Police (PNP) *carte blanche* to go after and kill drug lords, pushers, and addicts. He vowed to kill a million addicts if need be, in the same way that Adolf Hitler killed millions of Jews. . . . Duterte promised the police that he would protect them even from legal action, and police doubled their campaign. The extra-judicial killings proceeded in earnest, and by December 14, 2016, six months after Duterte was sworn in as president, 6,095 suspected drug addicts and pushers had already been killed by police special assassination teams and vigilantes.[42]

Cornelio and Medina point out that certain leaders and members of the Catholic Church started speaking up against Duterte, his bloody campaign against illegal drugs, and other contentious aspects of his presidency and remained undeterred despite Duterte issuing death threats and calling out Catholics, especially their leaders, for their hypocrisy.[43] Catholic, Protestant, and Evangelical leaders alike have pointed out that these extra-judicial killings have only been concentrated in poor communities while letting the wealthy drug lords run with impunity. The entire drug war was built on a blatant disregard for human rights and the rule of law, without any resolve to root out

---

[42] Abinales and Amoroso, *State and Society in the Philippines*, 340–341.
[43] Cornelio and Medina, "Christianity and Duterte's War on Drugs," 152.

the problem.⁴⁴ Despite these pronouncements, the church's voice of opposition is hardly a united front. However, it continues to grow as members of the church continually reflect on the call to respond to the challenge surfaced by Duterte's populism and his campaign against illegal drugs.

Given the Philippine church's involvement in the ouster of the late dictator Ferdinand Marcos, Sr., various groups, within and outside the Catholic Church, expect the hierarchy to be as outspoken as during the Marcos dictatorship. Some groups described the church's response during Duterte's presidency as lukewarm and tentative or, in some cases, absent.⁴⁵ Despite the perceived silence of some members of the church hierarchy, several priests like Frs. Robert Reyes, Flavie Villanueva, SVD, and Albert Alejo, SJ, have become vocal critics of Duterte's bloody anti-drug war. At the same time, other groups and individuals supported resistance movements by providing sanctuary to whistleblowers and potential witnesses against the drug war.⁴⁶ In fact, the Duterte administration filed charges of "conspiracy to commit sedition" against Alejo and Villanueva, together with other key personalities of the opposition, but these were eventually dropped.⁴⁷

Members and leaders of the Catholic Church who oppose Duterte do so either because of Duterte's campaign against illegal drugs or the challenge his brand of populism brings. Filipino theologian Jose Mario Francisco identifies how Duterte's populism has challenged the church and her evangelizing mission. Francisco is troubled with how Filipino Catholics and Christians show overwhelming support for Duterte's anti-drug campaign despite how it has systematically undermined due process, neglected human rights, and only targeted poor communities. He also mentions how the Catholic Church should reexamine its social mission, which entails working beyond the election season. It cannot be content having to "enjoin citizens in voting wisely, resisting patronage politics, and supporting [election] monitoring organizations."⁴⁸ Lastly, Francisco points out the need to challenge what he perceives to be a Manichean perspective implicit in Duterte's view of drug users and the drug problem in the Philippines.⁴⁹ At the heart of the last challenge posited by Francisco is an invitation

---

⁴⁴ Mario Francisco, SJ, "Challenges of Dutertismo to Philippine Christianity," *International Journal of Asian Christianity* 4 (2021): 153, doi.org/10.1163/25424246-04010008.
⁴⁵ Willis and Lopez, "Church vs. State," 47.
⁴⁶ Willis and Lopez, "Church vs. State," 52.
⁴⁷ Lian Buan, "Priests Plead Not Guilty to Sedition in 'Oust Duterte' Plot Charge," *Rappler*, October 20, 2020, www.rappler.com/nation/priests-plea-conspiracy-sedition-duterte-ouster-ploy-charge/.
⁴⁸ Francisco, "Challenges of Dutertismo to Philippine Christianity," 153.
⁴⁹ Francisco, "Challenges of Dutertismo to Philippine Christianity," 151.

for the church to grow in deeper recognition not just of those marginalized by Duterte's populism and anti-drug war but also those who have long been disenfranchised in Philippine society—the populist masses themselves.

THE CALL TO GROW IN RECOGNITION

In *The Moral Life*, his most recent book, Keenan outlines various stages to the moral life. The third of these foundational stages is recognition. Using Paddy McQueen's exposition on the unfolding of recognition, Keenan proposes that "the move from recognizing someone as familiar to giving recognition to one to whom it is due is, I think, the threshold into the moral life." This unfolding of recognition allows one to identify and acknowledge another person as a fellow human being, triggering our ethical responsiveness.[50] Overcoming populism requires that the various agents, as we have outlined above, grow in mutual recognition. Keenan suggests that the elites need to engage and recognize the populist masses.[51] Likewise, I would further suggest that populist masses are also called to acknowledge and recognize the humanity of the groups the populist leader touts as a threat to the masses' identity and security—the elites, drug users, and peddlers. In this way, the agency of the masses as populist supporters is not undermined.

First, we shall look into the importance of recognizing the humanity of the usual victims of Duterte's bloody drug war—the victims of extra-judicial killings, especially among the poor. Then, we shall consider how the church is called to greater vulnerability and recognition of those who have long experienced economic and political disenfranchisement within its own ranks.

A Church for Duterte's Scapegoats

When Cornelio and Medina studied how Christian communities responded to Duterte's anti-drug campaign, they noticed that the way communities responded was related to how they viewed the drug problem and drug users. Based on their study, religious communities would view them as "either sinful human beings or victims of wider social injustices such as poverty." These responses, however, are not necessarily mutually exclusive absolute categories.[52]

---

[50] James F. Keenan, *The Moral Life* (Washington, DC: Georgetown University Press, 2023), 41.
[51] Keenan, "Restoring Social Trust," 125.
[52] Cornelio and Medina, "Christianity and Duterte's War on Drugs," 154.

Some Christian and Catholic communities condemn the anti-drug campaign because it violates one of the commandments. Aside from this religious reason, others offer a nuanced view of the illegal drug problem that goes beyond treating it as a discipline and security concern. Several Catholic priests and their parish communities, especially in Payatas in Quezon City, a known hotspot for the anti-drug campaign, know that substance abuse is an issue of poverty and health rather than a mere criminal problem. This view is a far cry from seeing drug users only as obstinate sinners who need to be eradicated.[53] These differences in views, albeit positive, also inform the variety of responses. Some of these Christian communities help drug users and sellers by praying for their conversion, especially since they are convinced this is the only way a church should respond. Other church communities provide a comprehensive repertoire of interventions ranging from recollections and values formation programs to livelihood support, counseling, and legal assistance.[54]

One interesting result of Cornelio and Medina's study is that the Christian communities providing these comprehensive responses are motivated to do so not just because they have the resources but because of their immersion and engagement with these communities. Some of the priests and pastors of these churches live in areas known to be drug and extra-judicial killing hotspots. Cornelio and Medina point out that direct encounter with the "affected families has affirmed their theological understanding of drug users as victims of wider social injustices. The War on Drugs adds to the layers of injustices drug users already experience."[55] This response among Catholics and Christians reflects how the recognition of marginalized groups, especially of the scapegoats Duterte uses in his populist propaganda, leads to the ethical responsiveness of one collective to the plight of another. By being immersed and present to these communities, these leaders and the members of their congregations are, as Keenan writes, "vulnerably disposed to the other" which leads to their recognition of the drug war victims and eventually their discerned moral response in conscience.[56]

One of the vocal critics of Duterte's administration is Fr. Flavie Villanueva, SVD. Together with Fr. Albert Alejo, SJ, he was charged with conspiracy to commit sedition against the Duterte administration. However, he is also well-known for establishing the Arnold Janssen Kalinga Center in Tayuman, Manila, one of the hotspots of the drug campaign. The Kalinga Center caters to homeless people within the area, even those involved in the use and selling of drugs. Kalinga is an

---

[53] Cornelio and Medina, "Christianity and Duterte's War on Drugs," 159–160.
[54] Cornelio and Medina, "Christianity and Duterte's War on Drugs," 162–164.
[55] Cornelio and Medina, "Christianity and Duterte's War on Drugs," 166.
[56] Keenan, *The Moral Life*, 22.

acronym for *Kain, Ligo, Nang Ayos*, which means "to eat and take a bath with dignity."[57]

What is compelling about Fr. Flavie's story is that he himself used to be a drug addict before entering the seminary of the Society of Divine Word.[58] Their beneficiaries have witnessed the vigilante-style killings around their area, but they, together with the staff and benefactors of the Kalinga center, are convinced that the drug problem cannot be solved by killing the users and pushers. The homeless and Flavie himself are vulnerably disposed to recognizing these victims and the families they have left behind. They recognize that these people ended up as drug users partly due to the helplessness of having to deal with extreme poverty. However, some of the victims ended up as targets simply because they were poor and homeless, even if they had nothing to do with drugs. Thus, the Kalinga center caters to them as well and offers psychological support to those traumatized by the killings and other harassment brought about by Duterte's anti-drug campaign.[59]

A Church for Populist Masses

Lindsey Horner points out how there is a strong temptation to think of populist supporters as an uneducated mob and that the "liberal elite" are the educated ones. Even when evidence already points to the high support Duterte enjoyed from the middle and educated classes in Philippine society, most administration critics, including the vocal ones within the church, still stick with this narrative. Perpetuating this thinking cements any divide between the populist supporters and elites.[60] This temptation is often reinforced when one fails to recognize conflicting values and understanding of politics. Such conflicts can invite encounters and dialogue where mutual recognition, respect, and listening can be exercised.

In accounting for the unwavering support Duterte enjoyed, Curato reminds us that this comes from the vast majority of Filipinos excluded from the benefits of the country's economic gains over the past years. Thus, critics of Duterte should disabuse themselves of the notion that his supporters are morally compromised diehard fanatics who "call for killing sprees, scream bias at journalists, threaten rape

---

[57] "About Us—AJ Kalinga Foundation Inc," *Ajkalingafoundation.Org* (blog), accessed December 6, 2023, www.ajkalingafoundation.org/about-us/.
[58] Aika Rey, "From Drug Addiction to Priesthood," *Rappler*, accessed December 6, 2023, www.rappler.com/moveph/196880-drug-addiction-priesthood-faith-flavie-villanueva/.
[59] Rey, "From Drug Addiction to Priesthood."
[60] Lindsey K. Horner, "Oscillating between Populism and Liberalism in the Philippines: Participatory Education's Role in Addressing Stubborn Inequalities," *Globalisation, Societies, and Education* 22, no. 2 (2022), 3–4, doi.org/10.1080/14767724.2022.2048799.

and murder."[61] Amidst all these explanations, Curato offers another way of appreciating Duterte's supporters as people engaged in "constant negotiation between the politics of anxiety and the politics of hope."[62] That is why their understanding of good politics, as seen earlier, is defined more in terms of consideration and kindness rather than an elite understanding marked by transparency and accountability. Understanding these nuances does not come easily to most people unless there is a recognition of their hopes and frustrations brought about by encounters with them that makes elites, including church leaders, vulnerable, as Keenan would frame it.[63]

In presenting these, I am not suggesting that the church abandon its criticisms or prophetic role. As a matter of fact, in considering everything I have written thus far, I sense that the church, as a whole, is invited to deepen its commitment to mission, which Tuazon and Francisco also point out. If the Philippine church still believes it is called to be a church of the poor and for the poor, it needs to heed the call to greater vulnerability and recognition. Bishop Pablo Virgilio "Ambo" David, Bishop of the Diocese of Kalookan and President of the Catholic Bishops Conference of the Philippines (CBCP), can be seen as an exemplar in this regard. Ambo is one of those bishops who, Tony La Viña notes, "is not content to ensconce himself in the bishop's residence overseeing his diocese by way of remote control but is willing to sully his hands attending to the needs of his flock. . . . That is why he has made Kalookan a place of mission stations, bringing the church from the traditional parishes into the neighborhoods of the poor where most of the killings are happening."[64]

Mission stations, which started sprouting in Bishop Ambo's diocese, eventually became the fruit of the church's recognition of people marginalized both by society and the church. Rented houses in the middle of urban poor communities would become the residence of missionary priests or sisters. They would also serve as bases of operations for drug rehabilitation programs conducted in partnership with the local government and other civil society organizations.[65] As more and more priests and religious sisters lived in the same poor communities as their lay leaders and congregation, they would see and experience poverty and the problem of illegal drugs firsthand. Mission station chaplains noticed they began to understand better the poor and

---

[61] Curato, "Politics of Anxiety, Politics of Hope," 92.
[62] Curato, "Politics of Anxiety, Politics of Hope," 92.
[63] Keenan, *The Moral Life*, 24.
[64] Antonio La Viña, "[OPINION] Pablo Virgilio David: The Shepherd of Caloocan," *Rappler*, November 30, 2018, www.rappler.com/voices/thought-leaders/217859-bishop-pablo-virgilio-david-shepherd-caloocan/.
[65] "The Bishop Rehabilitating Caloocan," *ABS-CBN News*, accessed December 7, 2023, news.abs-cbn.com/ancx/culture/spotlight/11/23/18/the-bishop-rehabilitating-caloocan.

marginalized in their communities, and such "knowledge" would not just be attainable by quick sporadic visits. On the other hand, their presence has helped decrease incidents of violent encounters between gangs.[66]

These mission stations provide an immersive view of how relationships can be transformed by growing in vulnerability and recognition. In such a set-up, one can see the various agents mentioned earlier who can be found within the church—the elites, populist masses, and populists' scapegoats. In these neighborhoods, encounters can transform any anger, frustration, and resentment these agents may have with one another into a fruitful coexistence that, hopefully, goes beyond mere tolerance.

CONCLUSION

In this article, I have explored how populism is broadly understood as a nebulous concept, given the various causes that differ depending on the context. Yet one important characteristic is the antagonism amplified by the populist leader between two or more groups of citizens to garner popular support. In the case of the Philippines, the government's perceived inability to take decisive action in solving the problem of illegal drugs and the long history of disenfranchisement felt by the majority of Filipinos made the choice for an authoritarian populist like Duterte possible. Understanding the various agents embroiled in Duterte's populist regime also allowed us to understand the diversity of agencies within the Philippine church.

Despite how populism thrives with the fealty between supporters and the leader and the antagonistic relationship the masses have with elites and the populists' scapegoats, this cannot be the case for the Philippine church. Populism can be viewed as a challenge to the church's mission of recognizing and identifying itself with the poor and marginalized in society and even within its ranks. Otherwise, the history of disenfranchisement will continue even long after Duterte's presidency.

At the time of writing this article, Duterte no longer is president of the Philippines. Ferdinand Marcos, Jr., the late dictator's son, is the current president while Duterte's daughter, Sara Duterte, serves as vice-president. While the Marcos and Duterte camps are already planning for the subsequent election cycles, the government's drug war continues and seems to be just as bloody as during Duterte's time, despite Marcos's promise to pursue the campaign against illegal drugs

---

[66] Paul Jeffrey, "Taking the Church to the Peripheries: Mission Stations in Philippines | Franciscan Media," November 15, 2022, www.franciscanmedia.org/news-commentary/taking-the-church-to-the-peripheries-mission-stations-in-philippines/.

humanely.⁶⁷ Legislative hearings are being held to investigate Duterte's bloody drug war while the Philippine government still refuses to cooperate with the International Criminal Court's investigations on Duterte's drug war. Meanwhile, the masses continue to grumble at the inability of the elites to recognize their plight, dignity, and agency.

While this article makes a belated contribution to the discussion of Duterte's populism, I hope that the insights, reflections, and results of this research can help faith-based organizations and local church communities in refining their social advocacy programs, whether they are responding directly to the problem posed by the drug war or to the larger sources of disenfranchisement that have made Duterte's populist regime possible and still popular until today. Some of the ideas in this work may also be beneficial in other places where populism has become inimical to social advocacy, human rights, and faith communities. With the Catholic Church having just completed the Synod on Synodality, the call to continue to walk with God's people, especially the poor and disenfranchised, remains an urgent and constitutive part of proclaiming the Gospel. Given these considerations, the path to becoming a synodal church in the Philippines will require learning from the lessons offered by the populist challenge. Going on this journey requires the participation of the disenfranchised, recognizing them, as well as seeking ways of reparation and reconciliation that acknowledge the faults, hurts, and resentment of the various agents. Ⓜ

Edryan Paul J. Colmenares, SJ, is a Filipino Jesuit priest. He is pursuing his Licentiate in Sacred Theology, specializing in moral theology, at the Boston College Clough School of Theology and Ministry. His research interests include Catholic social teaching, political ethics, environmental ethics, and the formation of moral agents.

---

⁶⁷ Chris Fitzgerald, "Nothing Bloodless about Marcos, Jr.'s Drug War," *Asia Times*, July 31, 2024, www.asiatimes.com/2024/07/nothing-bloodless-about-marcos-jrs-drug-war/.

Reimagining Catholic Peacebuilding Through Pope Francis's "Culture of Encounter": The Case of Nigeria's Niger Delta Region

Martin Owhorchukwu Ejiowhor

Abstract: The document *Pacem in Terris* (PT) represents a pivotal moment in the history of Catholic social teaching, both at the level of the universal church and local churches. PT asserts that the church has a moral duty to contribute to global peace, to be founded on the principles of truth, justice, charity, and freedom, in imitation of Christ the Prince of Peace. This article argues that Pope Francis's "culture of encounter" (CoE) significantly advances this moral obligation, which it conceives as constitutive of the church's evangelizing mission, to contribute to sustainable just peace through social dialogue and active nonviolence incorporating well-coordinated peace advocacy while reimagining the conceptualization of conflict and peacebuilding processes. The article uses a literature review to examine two key questions: firstly, how Francis conceptualizes conflict in light of the CoE; and secondly, the practical implications of the CoE for rethinking Catholic peacebuilding strategies, especially in Nigeria's Niger Delta region. In conclusion, the article demonstrates how Pope Francis's papacy integrates teaching and praxis in the church's promotion of global peace. The "culture of encounter," a hallmark of Francis's papacy, calls for reinvigorated ecclesial self-identity and prophetic witness, essential for the church's active contribution to global conflict transformation and sustainable social peace.

TODAY, ABOUT A QUARTER OF HUMAN BEINGS LIVE IN PLACES plagued with the phenomenon of (violent) conflict, leaving over 84 million persons displaced globally.[1] For example, we have the Russian war in Ukraine, gun violence in the US, armed conflicts in Israel-Palestine, Syria, Afghanistan, Myanmar, Sudan, DRC, Mali, Haiti, Peru, Nigeria, etc. Some of these (violent) conflicts are linked to political power tussles, extremist religious ideologies, natural resource control, or a combination of many factors.

---

[1] UN Secretary-General António Guterres, "Remarks to Peacebuilding Commission on Sustainable Peacebuilding," (March 30, 2022), ww2.press.un.org/en/2022/sgsm2 1216.doc.htm#:~:text=As%20we%20%20meet%20today%2C%20one,violence%20 and%20human%20rights%20violations.

Nigeria's Niger Delta violent conflict is an example of a natural resource-based conflict, and it shall be discussed in detail as a case study in the last part of this article.

This multifocal reality of violence makes plain the fact that the promotion of peace is a global challenge that requires the collaboration of secular governments and religions. As a religious body, the Catholic Church engages in global peacebuilding through its institutions and teachings grounded in faith-inspired ideals and imaginations.[2] Examples of such teachings from the universal church and particular churches would include John XXIII's encyclical *Pacem in Terris* (PT), the African bishops' pastoral letter *Christ Our Peace* (2001), and the US bishops' pastoral letter *The Challenge of Peace* (1983, CP). These documents promote global peacebuilding as a moral duty binding for the church. Currently, Pope Francis's "culture of encounter" (CoE) carries forward this moral duty and, as I aim to show, reimagines it, thus taking the role of the Catholic Church in peacebuilding to the next level.

This article addresses the following three questions. First, how does Pope Francis conceive of conflict in light of the CoE? Second, what are the practical implications of the CoE for the Catholic Church's peacebuilding role? And third, how might these implications help us rethink the Nigerian Church's peacebuilding strategies in the Niger Delta region? To answer these questions, this article is divided into four sections. The first provides a contextual analysis of the Niger Delta violent conflict. The second section explores how Catholic social teaching conceived the church's peacebuilding role before Pope Francis. The third section conceptualizes the CoE and investigates how it reimagines the church's global peacebuilding role. The final section considers the implications of the CoE for rethinking the Nigerian Catholic Church's peacebuilding strategies in transforming the natural resource-based violent conflict in Nigeria's Niger Delta region.

Mapping the Niger Delta Violent Conflict

The Niger Delta region is situated in the southern part of Nigeria at the mouth of the river Niger, from where it derives its name, covering land and waterways inclusive of about seventy-five thousand square kilometers. Politically, the region comprises nine oil-producing states—Abia, Akwa Ibom, Bayelsa, Cross River, Delta, Edo, Imo, Ondo, and Rivers—that account for over forty-five million people

---

[2] See Maryann C. Love, *Global Issues: Beyond Sovereignty* (Lanham, MD: Rowman and Littlefield, 2020), 141–182.

with different spoken languages and cultural heritage.³ The peoples' means of livelihood and commercial activities are defined by the riverine and swampy as well as the mangrove forest terrain of the region, making it favorable for subsistent economies derived from fishing, farming, trading, food processing, and manufacturing. With the discovery of crude oil in commercial quantity in 1956, the Niger Delta region became the economic mainstay of Nigeria, with oil revenue accounting for over 60 and 80 percent of the nation's income and foreign exchange earnings respectively.⁴

However, the Niger Delta has been afflicted by violent conflict since the early 2000s, with the Nigerian government, multinational oil companies (MNCs), and Niger Delta militants as the principal conflict actors. Certain remote historical and political factors have been identified as causes of the violent conflict, such as the slave trade, colonialism, and unjust legislation.⁵ The Niger Delta became the largest outpost for the slave trade in West Africa due to the coastal nature of the region. The region has scarcely healed from the dehumanizing ordeal and trauma of the slave trade before the advent of British colonial rule.⁶ With the consolidation of its consular rule in the 1850s, the British exploited the Niger Delta people and their resources.⁷ For example, the colonial government enacted the Mineral Oil Act of 1914 which granted licenses and concessions for crude oil exploration and exploitation to British companies only.⁸ The

---

³ Due to the politics of oil and the revenue derivation policy associated with it, the Niger Delta region has been politically defined as comprising nine oil-producing states. This definition contrasts with the geographical cum cartographical as well as historical definition that recognizes Delta, Bayelsa, and Rivers as the three core states of the Niger Delta region (see Henry A. Daupamowei, "A Concise View of Niger Delta Region of Nigeria: An Interpretation of a Nigeria Historian," *International Research Journal of Interdisciplinary and Multidisciplinary Studies* 2, no. 10 [2016]: 56–63).

⁴ See Sabella O. Abidde, *Nigeria's Niger Delta: Militancy, Amnesty, and the Postamnesty Environment* (Lanham, MD: Lexington, 2017), 40. See also Ben Naanen, "When Extractive Governance Fails: Oil Theft as Resistance in Nigeria," *The Extractive Industries and Society* 6 (2019): 703; Cyril Obi and Siri Aas Rustad, "Introduction: Petro-violence in the Niger Delta—The Complex Politics of an Insurgency," in Cyril Obi and Siri Aas Rustad, eds., *Oil and Insurgency in the Niger Delta: Managing the Complex Politics of Petro-violence* (London: Zed, 2011), 3.

⁵ See Kekong Bisong, *Restorative Justice in Conflict Management* (Enugu: Snaap, 2008), 91–117.

⁶ Bisong, *Restorative Justice*, 91.

⁷ Tekena H. Tamuno, *Oil Wars in the Niger Delta 1849–2009* (Ibadan: Stirling-Horden, 2011), 19. See also Michael Odama, "Population Density and 'Slave Raiding': The Case of the Niger Delta of Nigeria," *Journal of African History* 10 (2005): 160.

⁸ John K. Wangbu, "Environmental and Social Cost of Oil in Nigeria: Niger Delta Agitation for Justice *vis-à-vis* Principles of Catholic Social Teaching," in John K. Wangbu, ed., *Niger Delta: Rich Region, Poor People* (Enugu: Snaap, 2005), 5.

colonialists brought together different kingdoms of the Niger Delta coast to create the Niger Coast Protectorate (NCP), but also merged the NCP with other kingdoms and ethnic groups that hitherto were not part of the Niger Delta coast to form the Southern Protectorate. The effect of this merger was worsened by the "unholy and unsolicited alliance" of 1914, in which the Southern and Northern Protectorates were amalgamated into one political entity called Nigeria, thereby marginalizing the region and obscuring its traditional autonomy and religious worldviews as well as cultural identity.[9]

Apart from the traumatizing effect of the slave trade and the negative impact of colonialism, the Niger Delta has also been a victim of unjust and unfavorable legal frameworks and policies.[10] Such laws include the reduction in revenue-sharing formula from 50 to 3 percent, but later raised to 13 percent in 1999; the 1978 Land Use Act (consolidated by the 2021 Petroleum Industry Act) which enabled the federal and state governments to claim ownership of land and resources in the Niger Delta; and discriminatory policies in Nigeria's political institutions. Particularly, the Land Use Act has been described as a gross injustice to the Niger Delta because it dislodged the Land Tenure System (LTS) that operated in the Niger Delta region and made all royalties, taxes, and rents paid to the state. The LTS was based on customary laws, which allowed families and communities to own land, while crude oil ownership was vested in the state. Most importantly, under the LTS arrangement, MNCs needed to obtain mining licenses from the state and permission from host communities before gaining access to the land for oil exploration and exploitation. The host communities received annual rent from the MNCs for permission and compensation for any damage to farm crops and plantation, property, or the land itself in the course of extractive activities.[11]

---

[9] Jonah I. Elaigwu, "Ethnicity and the Federal Option in Africa," *Nigerian Journal of Federalism* 1, no. 1 (1994): 69. Bisong argues that "the fundamental cause of the present Niger Delta crisis was laid in the colonial period within the context of the inability of the then government to address the issue of minorities. Minority in this perspective refers to an ethnic group who by virtue of their population are singled out from others and regard themselves as an object of collective discrimination. Therefore, a minority is bound to face exclusion from the political and economic life of the larger society. In this notion, the minority is in constant opposition with the dominant ethnic group" (Bisong, *Restorative Justice in Conflict Management*, 99; see also Louis Wirth, *The Problem of Minority Groups*, reprint [New York: Irvington, 1993]).

[10] Bisong, *Restorative Justice*, 104–105.

[11] See Kaniye S. A. Ebeku, "Oil and the Niger Delta People: The Injustice of the Land Use Act," *Verfassung und Recht in Übersee / Law and Politics in Africa, Asia, and Latin America* 35, no. 2 (2002): 201–231.

Additionally, proximate causes of the violent conflict have been identified. These include pollution and environmental degradation resulting from decades of oil exploration, which negatively impacts human health; the alienation and deprivation of the Niger Deltans from their resources, means of livelihood, and environment; unfair neglect by the government and MNCs; and socioeconomic and political marginalization and exclusion, leading to multidimensional poverty. These factors collectively contributed to the formation of the Niger Delta militant group and its subsequent demands for self-determination and control over the region's resources.[12] While the Niger Delta struggle commenced with peaceful intentions, aimed at transforming the region's adverse environmental, socio-economic, and political circumstances, its trajectory soon shifted towards violence. This transformation can be traced back to the Nigerian government's undiplomatic response and approach to the crisis at the heart of the movement.[13]

The Nigerian government has taken certain actions in response to the violent conflict and its subsequent impact on the nation's economy. These actions included some measures reflecting a militaristic initial approach employed to suppress the activities of the Niger Delta militants, preventing them from protesting and making demands. Instead of resolving the underlying issues in the region, this military response exacerbated the situation, causing significant distress and further conflict, as evidenced by reports of terror, rape, torture, and death, and the forcible displacement of many individuals whose villages were destroyed.[14] A typical example was the Ogoni crisis with Shell and the federal government, which led to the

---

[12] See Olalekan Bello, "The Dynamics of Nigeria's Oil and Gas Industry's Regulation: Revealing/Storying Neglected Voices and Excluded Lives of Environmental Encounters and Affects," (unpublished doctoral dissertation, University of Westminster, 2021); Emmanuel C. Onwuka, "Oil Extraction, Environmental Degradation and Poverty in the Niger Delta Region of Nigeria: A Viewpoint," *International Journal of Environmental Studies* 62, no. 6 (2006): 655–662; Eghosa E. Osaghae, Augustine Ikelegbe, Omobolaji O. Olarinmoye, and Stephen L. Okhomina eds., *Youth Militias, Self Determination, and Resource Control Struggle in the Niger Delta Region of Nigeria* (Dakar: CODESRIA, 2011); Zainab Mai-Bornu, "Oil, Conflict, and the Dynamics of Resource Struggle in the Niger Delta: A Comparison of the Ogoni and Ijaw Movements," *The Extractive Industries and Society* 6, no. 4 (2019): 1282–1291, w2.sciencedirect.com/science/article/pii/S2214790X19300863.

[13] See Fidelis A. E. Paki, "The Impact of Militarization of the Niger Delta Region of Nigeria," *Journal of Environmental Science and Resources Management* 11, no. 3 (2019): 1–18, w2.cenresinjournals.com/2020/06/09/the-impact-of-militarization-of-the-niger-delta-region-of-nigeria/.

[14] Emmanuel Osigwe, "Justice and Reconciliation in the Niger Delta of Nigeria: Exploring Insights from Catholic Social Thought," *Bulletin of Ecumenical Theology* 28 (2016): 60.

execution of human and environmental rights activist Ken Saro-Wiwa and eight others by the Nigerian military government in 1995. The second response was the establishment of intervention agencies and commissions, such as the Oil Mineral Producing Areas Development Commission (OMPADEC, 1992), the Niger Delta Development Commission (NDDC, 2000), the Ministry of Niger Delta Affairs (MNDA, 2008), and the Presidential Amnesty Programme (PAP, 2009). These commissions were established to address the underlying causes of the conflict, as well as to facilitate the development of human and infrastructure resources within the region. Although the PAP helped reduce the intensity of the violence because it invested in deradicalization and capital development of youth, these commissions have been unsuccessful in resolving the violent conflict in the region, which still experiences intermittent and sporadic physical violence. This failure has been attributed to their top-down approach, corruption, lack of strategic peacebuilding dialogue process, and lack of commitment on the part of the MNCs and Nigerian government.[15] Lastly, the government responded to the conflict by increasing the revenue derivation policy from 3 to 13 percent in 1999.[16] Despite the increase in revenue, Niger Deltans continued to suffer and the prospect of peace in the region remained elusive. This was due to a combination of factors, including a lack of expediency in the implementation process and the ultimate misappropriation of funds by corrupt politicians.[17] Additionally, militants in the Niger Delta have called for the reversal of the derivation policy, requesting a 50 percent revenue share, previously attainable when Nigeria's economy primarily relied on agricultural products from various regions of the country before the discovery of oil. The government's response to the conflict was unsuccessful because it could not alter the above-discussed fundamental unjust ecological, social, economic, and political structures, as well as the legal policies pertaining to land ownership

---

[15] See John K. Wangbu, *The Niger Delta Paradox: Impoverished in the Midst of Abundance* (Ibadan: Safari, 2018), 79–83.

[16] In the years following the country's independence (in 1960), the 1963 Republican Constitution maintained the status quo to the extent that the "1964 Binn Commission" continued to recommend a 50 percent allocation to the region where the revenue was generated. However, the distribution of revenues experienced fluctuations due to the government's reduction of the allocation to 5 percent in 1981 and 1.5 percent in 1984. Subsequently, the revenue was increased to 3 percent in 1992 and has remained at 13 percent since 1999. Bisong asserts that alterations to the derivative formula are predominantly influenced by individuals from the majority region, who have historically received 50 percent of the region's production prior to the discovery of oil in the Niger Delta (see Bisong, *Restorative Justice*, 104–105).

[17] Osigwe, "Justice and Reconciliation," 59–60.

and revenue sharing, which are the root causes of violence in the region.

Conscious of its moral duty to work for justice and promote social peace, and guided by the principles of CST, the Catholic Church in Nigeria has not been indifferent to the Niger Delta violent conflict. Through the Catholic Bishops Conference of Nigeria (CBCN), the church has responded to the violence by engaging in peacebuilding strategies such as issuing pastoral communiqués and charitable activities. In 2003, the church issued a communiqué at the end of its plenary meeting, condemning "the use of violence as a means to achieve any end, no matter how legitimate or noble."[18] It called all parties involved to dialogue, insisting that the government "set up a commission to identify the causes of the perennial violence, as well as those responsible and proffer an enduring solution to the crisis."[19] The church requested the Nigerian government and MNCs to "compensate and rehabilitate those who have suffered losses" as well as develop infrastructures (e.g., refineries, health care, education, housing, roads, etc.) in the region "in order to alleviate the suffering of the poor masses."[20] In 2006, at the end of its plenary, the church issued another communiqué in which it stated that the Niger Delta violent conflict resulting "principally from the long-standing social injustice against that region which contributes immensely to our national economy is regrettable."[21] As such, the church called on the government to "exercise utmost prudence in responding to the intermittent violence there."[22] The church has also carried out charitable activities in the region, such as almsgiving, capacity building in agro-business and climate-smart agriculture, and provision of medical services.[23] Despite

---

[18] CBCN, Communiqué "Hope for a Better Nigeria," Owerri, September 1–6, 2003, in Chris Anyanwu and Otunba J. Fadugba-Pinheiro, eds., *Our Concern for Nigeria: Catholic Bishops Speak: Communiqués Issued by the Catholic Bishops Conference on the State of the Church and Nigerian Nation from 1963 to 2015* (Abuja: Directorate of Social Communications, Catholic Secretariat of Nigeria, 2016): 210.

[19] CBCN, Communiqué "Hope for a Better Nigeria," 210.

[20] CBCN, Communiqué "Hope for a Better Nigeria," 210–211.

[21] CBCN, Communiqué "Keeping Hope Alive," Abuja, February 6–11, 2006, in Anyanwu and Fadugba-Pinheiro, eds., *Our Concern for Nigeria*, 234.

[22] CBCN, Communiqué "Keeping Hope Alive," 234.

[23] See Agenzia Fides, "The Church in Nigeria Collects Offerings for the Victims of Violence in the Niger Delta" (May 29, 2009), w2.fides.org/en/news/24345-africa_nigeria_the_church_in_nigeria_collects_offerings_for_the_victims_of_violence_in_the_niger_delta_it_is_not_time_to_apportion_blames_but_to_assist_our_brothers_and_sisters_in_need; Catholic Caritas Foundation of Nigeria (CCFN), "Youth in Farming Business" (2015–2016), w2.caritasnigeria.org/index.php?option=com_mtree&task=listcats&cat_id=86&Itemid=1081; CCFN, "Emergency Response" (June 2018), w2.caritasnigeria.org/index.php?option=com_mtree&task=viewlink&link_id=52&Itemid=1082; CCFN, "Support for Vaccine Justice in Nigeria Using Faith-Based Leaders"

the successes recorded by the church's strategies of issuing communiqués and engaging in charitable actions, it could not transform the Niger Delta violent conflict due to some pitfalls in its strategies, discussed later in this article. Hence, there is a need to rethink the church's peacebuilding strategies in light of Francis's culture of encounter peacebuilding model.

CATHOLIC PEACEBUILDING BEFORE POPE FRANCIS

In order to gain insight into the culture of encounter and its peacebuilding model, it is essential to examine Catholic peacebuilding before Francis's pontificate. The idea of peacebuilding in Catholic social teaching flows from the biblical vision of positive peace, classified into three dimensions, namely eschatological (fulfillment of creation), spiritual (interior peace), and political (proper ordering of and right relations in society) peace.[24] Although the primary vocation of the church might be to bring about spiritual and eschatological peace, the Catholic Church has not been indifferent to contributing to political peace through its social teaching because it believes that the three dimensions of peace are interconnected.[25] Most especially in the modern period, beginning with the encyclical *Rerum Novarum* (1891) of Leo XIII, the church has taken its duty to contribute to political peace more seriously. Since then, the church at the universal and local levels has continued to progress amid challenges in this global peacebuilding agenda.

The year 1963 represents a watershed moment in the development of official Catholic social teaching, especially on peace and war, as it was the year John XXIII issued the encyclical *Pacem in Terris* (Peace on Earth) addressed, for the first time in the history of papal encyclicals, to all Catholics and people of good will to emphasize our collective responsibility towards building global peace. PT claims that peace is an objective desire of every human being: "For who is there who does not feel the craving to be rid of the threat of war, and to see peace preserved and made daily more secure?"[26] It argues that global peace "can never be established, never guaranteed, except by the diligent observance of the divinely established order" (PT, no. 1). The

---

(January–December 2022), w2.caritasnigeria.org/index.php?option=com_mtree&task= viewlink&link_id=86&Itemid=271.
[24] Kenneth R. Himes, "Peacebuilding and Catholic Social Teaching," in Robert J. Schreiter, Scott R. Appleby, and Gerard F. Powers, eds., *Peacebuilding: Catholic Theology, Ethics, and Praxis* (New York: Orbis Books, 2010): 268–269.
[25] Himes, "Peacebuilding and Catholic Social Teaching," 269.
[26] John XXIII, *Pacem in Terris*, no. 115, w2.vatican.va/content/john-xxiii/en/encyclicals/ documents/hf_j-xxiii_enc_11041963_pacem.html (PT hereafter).

church bears the responsibility to facilitate the formation of individual consciences through an "integral education" that equips them with the capacity to construct a peace founded upon the principles of truth, justice, charity, and freedom (PT, nos. 153 and 167).

PT conceives peacebuilding as "both [a] divine and human task," which "marks the beginning of a new understanding of Christians' vocation to promote peace."[27] This new understanding is grounded in the person of Christ who is both the "Author of Peace" and "Prince of Peace" (PT, nos. 117 and 166) and in the promotion and protection of equality of human rights, knowing that "without respect for human rights, peace cannot be reliably sustained."[28] What underlies equality of rights and duties, be it economic, religious, political, moral, or cultural, is the principle of human dignity (PT, nos. 20, 35, 104, and 122). Also, PT understands peace not as mere tranquility in society or the absence of war but as a constant effort to maintain harmony in human relationships based on respect for human rights and mutual trust.[29]

That peacebuilding requires constant effort is an indication that building sustainable and dynamic social peace is a process. Vatican II's *Gaudium et Spes* (GS hereafter) attests that "peace is never attained once and for all, but must be built up ceaselessly" in society through sincere collaborative efforts of all global citizens and institutions.[30] As a universal institution, in obedience to the truth of the Gospel of Christ, GS invites all Christians and people of good will "to do in love what the truth requires, and to join with all true peacemakers in pleading for peace and bringing it about" (GS, no. 78).

Taking this invitation both in PT and GS seriously, different local Catholic churches at the continental, regional, and national levels have reflected on the peacebuilding mission of the church based on their context and particularities. At the continental level, for example, the African bishops published a pastoral letter, entitled "Christ Our Peace," in 2001. This document was the final outcome of the Plenary Assembly of SECAM in 2000, and reflected on the Church's peacebuilding mission. The document states that in Africa and the world at large, violence and wars are mostly the result of an unjust political, social, and economic system that creates inequality, and the

---

[27] Laurie Johnston, "*Pacem in Terris* and Catholic Peacebuilding," *Journal of Catholic Social Thought* 11, no. 1 (2014): 94.
[28] Johnston, "*Pacem in Terris*," 96.
[29] Johnston, "*Pacem in Terris*," 96.
[30] Second Vatican Council, "*Gaudium et Spes*: Pastoral Constitution on the Church in the Modern World," no. 78), w2.vatican.va/archive/hist_councils/ii_vatican_council/documents/vat-ii_const_19651207_gaudium-et-spes_en.html (GS hereafter).

church must speak against and work to transform such a system.³¹ It argues that "the Church as a family of God" must be "at the service of the peace that Christ offers humanity," and the church carries out this service "particularly through catechesis and through various diplomatic initiatives for peace."³² The church's peace catechesis and initiatives must place a premium on the necessity of conversion and dialogue to advance the causes of justice, forgiveness, and reconciliation; to promote appropriate human relationships with God and one another; and foster recognition and respect for human dignity and human rights.³³

The need for conversion and dialogue to promote the values of justice and reconciliation necessary for sustainable and dynamic peacebuilding was especially highlighted during the Second African Synod of Bishops on "The Church in Africa in Service to Reconciliation, Justice, and Peace" in 2009. The Synod fathers argued that "the Church in Africa, both as a family of God and as individual faithful has the duty to be instruments of peace and reconciliation, after the heart of Christ, who is our peace and reconciliation."³⁴ They maintained that breaking the vicious cycle of violence does not admit unforgiveness, revenge, or counterattack but requires forgiveness grounded in the admission of wrongdoing, reparation, justice, and solidarity capable of promoting "peace that goes to the roots of the conflict."³⁵ The Synod fathers called on all the dioceses in Africa as "artisans of peace and reconciliation" to prioritize the peacebuilding agenda by establishing the Justice and Peace Commission and instilling in its members and institutions the values of justice, forgiveness, reconciliation, transparency, accountability, and common good to mitigate poverty and promote peace.³⁶

At the national level, the Nigerian Catholic Bishops issued a pastoral communiqué on "Peace Through Justice and Love" in 1989.³⁷

---

³¹ Symposium of Episcopal Conferences of Africa and Madagascar (SECAM hereafter), Pastoral Letter "Christ Our Peace [Eph 2:14]: The Church-as-Family of God, Place and Sacrament of Pardon, Reconciliation, and Peace in Africa" (Kumasi: Catholic Press, 2001), nos. 26–32.
³² SECAM, "Christ Our Peace," no. 61.
³³ SECAM, "Christ Our Peace," nos. 57–60 and 65–67.
³⁴ Second African Synod of Bishops, "Message to the People of God of the Second Special Assembly for Africa of the Synod of Bishops," (October 23, 2009), no. 8, w2.vatican.va/roman_curia/synod/documents/rc_synod_doc_20091023_message-synod_en.html.
³⁵ Second African Synod of Bishops, "Message to the People of God," nos. 8–9.
³⁶ Second African Synod of Bishops, "Message to the People of God," nos. 18–27.
³⁷ Catholic Bishops Conference of Nigeria (CBCN hereafter), "Peace Through Justice and Love" (1989), in Anyanwu and Fadugba-Pinheiro, eds., *Our Concern for Nigeria*, 65–71.

The bishops stated that it is a "God-given mission to work relentlessly and in faith" for the promotion of peace within the church and society built on justice, truth, love, and universal brotherhood.[38] For them, "true religion has to do with God who is one, true, just, and loving. It cannot lead to disunity, deceit, injustice, and hatred."[39] As such, the church as a religious body has to "fight against injustice and evil, wherever it is found, and to promote [common] goodness and justice" vital to building sustainable peace in society.[40] However, the bishops acknowledged that peacebuilding is challenging, but they argued that the church must arm itself with the weapons of dialogue, Christian solidarity, and collaboration with other religious and secular groups to challenge unjust structures at the social, economic, and political levels to promote social peace.[41]

Despite these contributions of the church at various levels, achieving global peacebuilding in our contemporary time remains a challenge that calls for much more ecclesial commitment. Pope Francis appears to take seriously this challenge, inviting the church to reimagine its peacebuilding project through the practice of a culture of encounter.

POPE FRANCIS AND THE REIMAGINATION OF CATHOLIC PEACEBUILDING

The ongoing pontificate of Pope Francis has shown itself to be carrying forward and reimagining the Catholic global peacebuilding project. However, a proper analysis of the extent of this Catholic peacebuilding reimagination requires an understanding of the notion of "culture of encounter" (CoE), which has become a defining mark and dominant idea of Francis's pontificate as it runs through almost all his writings, addresses, homilies, etc. I shall focus primarily on *Evangelii Gaudium* (EG),[42] *Laudato Si'* (LS),[43] and *Fratelli Tutti* (FT)[44] to examine how Pope Francis conceives of this notion and uses it to carry forward and reimagine the church's global peacebuilding agenda.

---

[38] CBCN, "Peace Through Justice and Love," 65.
[39] CBCN, "Peace Through Justice and Love," 66.
[40] CBCN, "Peace Through Justice and Love," 66.
[41] CBCN, "Peace Through Justice and Love," 67–70.
[42] Pope Francis, *Evangelii Gaudium* (November 24, 2013), w2.vatican.va/content/fran cesco/en/apost_exhortations/documents/papa-francesco_esortazione-ap_20131124_e vangelii-gaudium.html.
[43] Pope Francis, *Laudato Si'* (May 24, 2015), w2.vatican.va/content/francesco/en/en cyclicals/documents/papa-francesco_20150524_enciclica-laudato-si.html.
[44] Pope Francis, *Fratelli Tutti* (October 3, 2020), w2.vatican.va/content/francesco/ en/encyclicals/documents/papa-francesco_20201003_enciclica-fratelli-tutti.html.

The Culture of Encounter and Ecclesial Conversion

In *Evangelii Gaudium*, Pope Francis uses the concept of "encounter" apropos of the person of Jesus, arguing that our encounter with Jesus leads us to encounter others in their infinite dignity and "desire, seek, and protect the good of [these] others" (EG, nos. 1–3 and 178). Such an encounter with Jesus and otherness is understood primarily as "an event . . . which gives life a new horizon and a decisive direction" (EG, no. 7). The strong desire to seek the good of others flows from "God's love, which blossoms into an enriching friendship" with others (EG, no. 8). "For if we have received the love which restores meaning to our lives, how can we fail to share that love with others" (EG, no. 8) and thus seek their good?

In *Laudato Si'*, Pope Francis extends the notion of encounter from an encounter with God and a "generous encounter between persons" (LS, no. 47) to include encounter with the natural world, noting that the effects of people's encounter with God "become evident in their relationship with the world around them" (LS, no. 217). Why? Because a genuine encounter includes, among other things, being in fraternal "contact with nature" since "encountering God does not mean fleeing from this world or turning our back on nature" (LS, nos. 223 and 235). Rather, a genuine encounter with God calls for "an integral ecology" that "shows us just how inseparable the bond is between concern for nature, justice for the poor, commitment to society, and interior peace" (LS, no. 10). For Pope Francis, the practice of integral ecology is possible if human beings are willing to undergo or experience "an ecological conversion" (LS, no. 217).

Like LS, *Fratelli Tutti* expands the circle of encounter. Addressed to "all people of goodwill" (FT, no. 6) it is thus more inclusive. Pope Francis writes: "To speak of a culture of encounter means that we, as a people, should be passionate about meeting others, seeking points of contact, building bridges, and planning a project that includes everyone" in such a manner that it "becomes an aspiration and a style of life" (FT, no. 216). With the practice of the CoE, our society becomes "capable of transcending our differences and divisions" to build a "society where differences coexist, complementing, enriching, and reciprocally illuminating one another, even amid disagreements and reservations" (FT, no. 215).

The culture of encounter can take place at interpersonal/group and social/societal levels to create "a new vision of fraternity and social friendship" (FT, no. 6). At the interpersonal/group level, the goal is conversion that includes "ecological conversion" (LS, no. 217) and ecclesial and missionary conversion to transform the church's evangelizing mission, which has implications for the church's self-identity and prophetic witnessing (EG, nos. 25–26). At the social level, the goal is to "contribute to the promotion of justice and peace within communities and among nations on the global level" by creating "more sound institutions, more just regulations, more supportive structures."[45] The goal is to contribute to a "genuine and lasting peace" (FT, no. 217) via a process that empowers people to embrace differences and work for "a reconciled diversity" as well as recognize the value of every person and non-human creation (EG, no. 230). This process is founded on the values of human dignity, justice, love, and solidarity and uses social dialogue—"approaching, speaking, listening, looking at, coming to know and understand one another and to find common ground" (FT, no. 198)—as a mechanism of peacebuilding.

To this end, Pope Francis outlines his now-familiar four principles important for re-envisaging the processes of peacebuilding and the common good in society (EG, nos. 217–237). The first principle—"time is greater than space"—inculcates the virtue of patience able to overcome challenges in peacebuilding (EG, no. 223). This initial tenet recognizes the exasperation experienced by those engaged in the peacebuilding process, particularly the perceived loss of time due to the complex nature of the process.[46] The second principle—"unity prevails over conflict"—points to the reality of and human attitudes toward conflict: those who ignore or conceal conflict, those who embrace it wrongly and become its prisoners, and those who confront it head-on. The pope considers the latter category of people as peacebuilders because they make it "possible to build communion amid disagreement" and "go beyond the surface of the conflict . . . to see others in their deepest dignity" (EG, nos. 227–228). This principle calls for the virtue of courage and the willingness to confront differences since conflicts ought not to "be the occasion for fear, but rather the occasion for moral greatness."[47] The third principle—"realities are more important than ideas"—invites all to anchor peace proposals on practical and feasible realities and reject abstractions (EG, no. 231). For Francis, words or ideas bereft of actions become idealism that leads nowhere and simply changes nothing but deteriorates the status quo (EG, no. 232). With this principle, Francis seems to chastise otherworldly Christians (detached from real human experience) and contrast the logic of intellectualism with the fruitfulness of the logic of practice, such as promoting justice and

---

[45] David Hollenbach, "Religious Nationalism, a Global Ethic, and the Culture of Encounter," *Theological Studies* 83, no. 3 (2022): 376.
[46] Bernard V. Brady, *Essential Catholic Social Thought*, 2nd edition (New York: Orbis Books, 2017), 293.
[47] Brady, *Essential Catholic Social Thought*, 294.

works of mercy.⁴⁸ Lastly, the final principle—"the whole is greater than the part"—calls for the constant broadening of horizons in our thinking and actions for the benefit of all (EG, nos. 234–235). As such, the principle does not admit a single perspective that fails to see the larger picture because the different parts of reality are needed to keep the good of their particularity. Nevertheless, the whole is equally essential for the pursuit of the common good. Pope Francis beautifully describes the convergence of the different parts of reality without losing sight of the distinctive character of each part with the image of the "polyhedron" (EG, no. 236).

With these principles, Pope Francis indicates that peacebuilding as a process is challenging but achievable if we face one another, not as enemies but as brothers and sisters endowed with dignity, and the tensions that result from unhealthy relationships with courage, patience, mercy, justice, and solidarity rather than being indifferent to social conflicts, excluding or discarding others. Thus, the CoE prioritizes and reimagines Catholic peacebuilding but denounces the culture of throw-away (EG, no. 53), global indifference (EG, no. 54), and exclusion (EG, nos. 53 and 59), which rejects God, ethics, and solidarity.⁴⁹

Under the papacy of Pope Francis, global peacebuilding is no longer merely an appendix to Catholic moral duties but constitutive of the evangelizing mission of a church that "goes forth" to encounter other cultures (EG, no. 20).⁵⁰ His culture of encounter calls for ecclesial and missionary conversion. This has implications for the church and its evangelizing mission, such as peacebuilding. According to Catherine Clifford, there are three goals or implications to ecclesial conversion.⁵¹ First, ecclesial conversion calls for "a return to the kerygmatic proclamation of faith" and witness; second, it aims at grounding this renewed kerygmatic proclamation and prophetic

---

⁴⁸ Brady, *Essential Catholic Social Thought*, 294–295.

⁴⁹ Pope Francis, "Address to the New Non-Resident Ambassadors to the Holy See: Kyrgyzstan, Antigua and Barbuda, Luxembourg, and Botswana" (May 16, 2013), w2.vatican.va/content/francesco/en/speeches/2013/may/documents/papa-francesco_20130516_nuovi-ambasciatori.html; Alexandru Taşnadi, Iustin E. Alexandru, Gheorghe Ustinescu, and Petru C. Bradu, "Consumerism and Exclusion in a Throw-Away Culture," *Theoretical and Applied Economics* 25, no. 3 (2018): 101–112.

⁵⁰ Pope Francis, *Praedicate Evangelium* (March 19, 2022), Art. 165, w2.vatican.va/content/francesco/en/apost_constitutions/documents/20220319-costituzione-ap-praedicate-evangelium.html.

⁵¹ Catherine E. Clifford, "Pope Francis's Call for the Conversion of the Church in Our Time," in Stephen van Erp and Karim Schelkens, eds., *Conversion and Church: The Challenge of Ecclesial Renewal: Essays in Honour of H. P. J. Witte* (Leiden: Brill, 2016): 147–177.

witnessing spiritually; and third, it envisions the conversion of the church's institutions and structures to reflect its new self-identity and render its Gospel proclamation and witnessing more effective to the world.[52] A new ecclesial self-identity means that the church becomes a merciful church (EG, nos. 193–194), inclusive by being "poor and for the poor" (EG, no. 198), reaching out to those on the fringes of society (EG, nos. 20–24), and more dialogical and pastoral in its activities rather than hyper-juridical.[53] Mercy is conceived not just as the identity of the church but also as the foundation and end of its mission.[54] One concrete example of how the church could express this logic of mercy is by prioritizing a nonviolent approach in its mission of transforming social violence and building sustainable just peace.[55] Such expression of self-identity and mission, grounded in mercy, has implications. It calls the church to be prophetic in its witness to the world. A prophetic church engages in social witness by being dialogically discerning in its activities, participating and engaging in sacred and social issues for the integral good of God's creation, and embodying in its structures and institutions the very values and principles it advocates, such as mercy, human dignity, human rights, justice, equality, inclusiveness, and peace.[56]

Both a renewed self-identity and prophetic witness are vital to the church's social mission. As such, the CoE refocuses the church's social mission as peacebuilding for "a better world"; this must go beyond mere "charitable and educational activities" (FT, no. 276) to concrete group actions grounded in mercy but actively "effectuated in the struggle for justice" at both interpersonal and structural levels, interrogating the socioeconomic, political, and ecological structures.[57] This mission requires ethical imagination and principles drawn from the Gospel and human sciences. For instance, understanding the socioeconomic and political realities of those in conflict and the causes underlying the conflict is the first valuable step that must be taken when engaging in a peacebuilding project. Also, recourse to

---

[52] Clifford, "Pope Francis's Call," 147–148.

[53] Pope Francis, "Address at the Commemorative Ceremony for the 50th Anniversary of the Synod of Bishops" (October 17, 2015), w2.vatican.va/content/francesco/en/speeches/2015/october/documents/papa-francesco_20151017_50-anniversario-sinodo.html.

[54] Leo Guardado, "Nonviolence: The Witness of a Church of Mercy," *Expositions* 13, no. 2 (2019): 57.

[55] Guardado, "Nonviolence," 62.

[56] Kristin E. Heyer, *Prophetic and Public: The Social Witness of US Catholicism* (Washington, DC: Georgetown University Press, 2006), 188–199.

[57] Martin Ejiowhor, "Pope Francis's Culture of Encounter as a Paradigm Shift in the Magisterium's Reception of Justice in the World," *Journal of Catholic Social Thought* 18, no. 2 (2021): 208.

militarization and coercive pressure or cajolery via unreasonable sanctions has never been fruitful and can hardly build sustainable peace. It is diametrically opposed to ecclesial peacebuilding which aims to "build lasting, sustainable, inclusive peace, both to prevent violence and, once violence has broken out, to restore a more robust peace" by engaging in a genuine, bottom-up, inclusive, and participatory dialogue process among conflict actors.[58]

For example, the Colombian Catholic Church established the National Conciliation Commission (CCN) to facilitate conflict transformation and peacebuilding dialogue processes between the Colombian government and various armed groups, such as the Revolutionary Armed Forces of Colombia (FARC), the National Liberation Army (ELN), and the United Self-Defence Forces (AUC), to resolve the decades-long resource-based armed conflict in Colombia. The church adopted a community-based pastoral dialogue approach that involved empathic listening, accompaniment, forgiveness, and reconciliation. These peace dialogue efforts led to the 2016 Colombian peace agreement.[59] Also, the Sant' Egidio Community, a Rome-based religious NGO group, facilitated a peacebuilding dialogue process to resolve the post-colonial Mozambican civil war between the FRELIMO (the ruling party) and RENAMO (anti-government militant group), leading to the signing of the General Peace Agreement in 1992.[60]

The examples of the Colombian Catholic Church and Sant' Egidio's use of dialogue as a peacebuilding mechanism in Colombia and Mozambique, respectively, confirm Pope Francis's emphasis on social dialogue as the best "weapon" the church possesses for global peacebuilding. Moreover, peacebuilding is a process and not a one-time event or exercise. To facilitate such a peacebuilding dialogue process, Francis challenges the church to undergo its own conversion to become credible to those it facilitates in dialogue processes: be patient enough to overcome the frustration associated with such a project; be courageous to interrogate socioeconomic, political, and ecological injustices underlying any conflict and capable of hindering meaningful peacebuilding efforts; broaden horizons of imagination and actions and be dynamic enough to engage an integrative

---

[58] Maryann C. Love, "Just Peace and Just War," *Expositions* 12, no. 1 (2018): 61.
[59] See John Paul Lederach, "The Long Journey Back to Humanity: Catholic Peacebuilding with Armed Actors," in Schreiter, Appleby, and Powers, eds., *Peacebuilding: Catholic Theology, Ethics, and Praxis*, 23–55.
[60] Andrea Bartoli, Aldo Civico, and Leone Gianturco, "Mozambique–Renamo," in Bruce W. Dayton and Louis Kriesberg, eds., *Conflict Transformation and Peacebuilding: Moving from Violence to Sustainable Peace* (New York: Routledge, 2009), 140–155.

peacebuilding approach that involves both formal and cultural dialogue where necessary; and ensure it adopts a peacebuilding approach that is practicable and resonates with realities and experiences of conflict actors and those directly affected by the conflict. The church must promote the conversion dimension of social dialogue, for there could be a resurgence of conflict where such attitudinal conversion is lacking among the dialogue partners. Finally, the CoE challenges the church to ensure that the dialogue process is inclusive and participatory, free from gender biases and age discrimination. The church's goal is to build sustainable peace on the foundation of truth, respect for human dignity and human rights, care for the environment, justice, and mercy (the willingness to give and receive forgiveness).

The Culture of Encounter Reimagines Catholic Peacebuilding

Given this ecclesial conversion, the question then becomes: how does Pope Francis's CoE carry forward and reimagine the church's global peacebuilding agenda inaugurated in PT? In what follows, I shall attempt to answer this question.

Pope Francis carries forward John XXIII's call for global peace in PT, considering that he refers to PT's peace vision in his documents. In LS, for example, Francis refers to how PT, addressed not only to Catholics but to all people of good will, "rejected war but offered a proposal for peace" (LS, no. 3). He goes on to state that in a similar manner his message for integral ecology, which entails peaceful and harmonious relationships among creation, is being addressed to "every human person living on this planet" (LS, no. 3). In FT, Francis reiterates PT's call for peace, based on the fact that "it no longer makes sense to maintain that war is a fit instrument with which to repair the violation of justice" (PT, no. 127), insisting that "arguments for peace are stronger than any calculation of particular interests and confidence in the use of weaponry" (FT, no. 206). Francis strongly believes that PT invites "renewed progress in . . . the development of peacebuilding initiatives" so that people can coexist as brothers and sisters and flourish together as John XXIII earnestly hoped for in PT.[61]

Although it rejects violence in all shades, the CoE peacebuilding model appears to have a positive conception of conflict in contrast to what has been, such as in PT. This model of peacebuilding conceives social conflict as calling attention to a positive way of reconciling underlying contradictory human needs, values, and interests in human

---

[61] Pope Francis, "Message to Mark the Conference on *Pacem in Terris* Organized by the Academy of Social Sciences" (September 12, 2023), w2.vatican.va/content/francesco/en/messages/pont-messages/2023/documents/20230912-messaggio-60annipaceminterris.html.

relationships. In his address to the Eucharistic Youth Movement in 2015, Pope Francis argues that "when there is life, there is tension and there is conflict" and that social conflict "can also do us good, for they make us understand differences, and make us understand that if we do not find a way to resolve this conflict, there will be a situation of war."[62] Here, Pope Francis calls not only the youth but the entire church to embrace and transform social conflict. He believes that "only what is embraced is transformed" and calls on the church to embrace the reality of social conflicts and commit much effort to transform them, knowing that "the miracle of the culture of encounter" is experienced when bridges are built and peace is attained.[63] This clarion call resonates with Francis's second peacebuilding principle ("unity prevails over conflict") which, as mentioned earlier, calls for the "willingness to face conflict head-on, to resolve it, and to make it a link in the chain of a new process," thereby making it "possible to build communion amid disagreement" (EG, nos. 227–228). Thus, in the CoE peacebuilding model, conflict could be strategic and constructive, especially when it is a temporary but "necessary disruption that enables deeper inter-party unity and cooperation in the future."[64] An example of such constructive conflict is active nonviolence, which adopts strategies such as civil resistance and nonviolent mass protest that are momentarily disruptive but aim at transforming direct, structural, and cultural violence to foster positive peace.

Francis's CoE peacebuilding model seems to prioritize and advocate a just peace approach without completely dismissing the just war tradition, a dominant approach in Catholic peacebuilding, on the grounds of "the injustice of war" (FT, no. 256).[65] Just peace is defined as "the mutually constitutive and interactive commitment to and

---

[62] Pope Francis, "Address to the Eucharistic Youth Movement" (August 7, 2015), w2.vatican.va/content/francesco/en/speeches/2015/august/documents/papa-francesco_20150807_meg.html.

[63] Pope Francis, *Christus Vivit* (March 25, 2019), nos. 120 and 169, w2.vatican.va/content/francesco/en/apost_exhortations/documents/papa-francesco_esortazione-ap_20190325_christus-vivit.html.

[64] Véronique Dudouet, "Nonviolent Resistance in Power Asymmetries," in B. Austin, M. Fischer, and H. J. Giessmann, eds., *Advancing Conflict Transformation* (Opladen: Barbara Budrich, 2011), 256.

[65] Pope Francis strongly questions the concept of just war, and he seems to invite us to do so. He says: "To the explicit rejection of my predecessors, the events of the first two decades of this century compel me to add, unambiguously, that there is no occasion in which a war can be considered just. There is never a place for the barbarism of war, especially not when contention acquires one of its most unjust faces: that of so-called 'preventive wars'" ("War Must End or World Risks Nuclear Catastrophe," *Vatican News*, October 16, 2022, w2.vaticannews.va/en/pope/news/2022-10/pope-francis-book-10th-anniversary-pontificate.html).

pursuit of social cohesion and equity, in both orientation or aim and action."[66] The ethics of just peace, according to Lisa Cahill, "stresses nonviolent conflict transformation, strategies of nonviolent resistance, the frequently disingenuous and excessive nature of even 'just' uses of violence, and the ongoing processes required to attain just and sustainable peace."[67] For Cahill, just peace can offer the church an alternative approach to just war theory and strict pacifism, considering that both latter approaches present us with a kind of "moral dilemma."[68] Cahill observes that both just war tradition and pacifism present us with moral dilemmas. She argues that, even if some instances of war appear to have a just cause, the action of killing another violates human dignity. For example, there is a growing scientific recognition of perpetrator-induced trauma and a process of dehumanization of victims by their killers, a process that obstructs their capacity to show empathy.[69] Similarly, strict pacifism renounces totally the use of force to stop an unjust aggressor from killing the innocent, thereby potentially placing the pacifist in "a position of complicity with grievous evils perpetrated against the innocent."[70] Cahill notes that although this moral dilemma "may be impossible to resolve satisfactorily," just peace presents an alternative approach of "protecting the innocent and creating peace with justice without resorting to killing."[71]

This reasoning on just peace resonates with Pope Francis. He states: "No war is just. The only just thing is peace."[72] In his message to participants of the 2016 Rome conference on "Nonviolence and Just Peace," he notes that "the basic premise is that the ultimate and most deeply worthy goal of human beings and of the human community is the abolition of war."[73] Further, he chose "Nonviolence: A Style of

---

[66] Love, "Just Peace and Just War," 60–61.
[67] Lisa S. Cahill, "Just War, Pacifism, Just Peace, and Peacebuilding," *Theological Studies* 80, no. 1 (2019): 171.
[68] Lisa S. Cahill, "The Changing Vision of 'Just Peace' in Catholic Social Tradition," *Journal of Moral Theology* 7, no. 2 (2018): 106.
[69] See Erin McGlothlin, "Perpetrator Trauma," in *Routledge Companion to Literature and Trauma*, ed. Colin Davis and Hanna Meretoja (New York: Routledge, 2020), 100–110; Jack Pemment, "Dissecting Empathy: How Do Killers Experience Other People?," *Psychology Today* (September 19, 2013), w2.psychologytoday.com/us/blog/blame-the-amygdala/201309/dissecting-empathy.
[70] Cahill, "The Changing Vision of 'Just Peace,'" 106.
[71] Cahill, "The Changing Vision of 'Just Peace,'" 107.
[72] Pope Francis and Dominique Wolton, *The Path to Change: Thoughts on Politics and Society* (London: Pan Macmillan, 2018), 27.
[73] Pope Francis, "Message to Card. Peter K. A. Turkson on the Occasion of 'Nonviolence and Just Peace: Contributing to the Catholic Understanding of and Commitment to Nonviolence'" (April 11–13, 2016), w2.vatican.va/content/francesco

Politics for Peace" as the theme for his 2017 World Day of Peace Message. In the message, Francis writes: "Especially in situations of conflict, let us respect this, our 'deepest dignity,' and make active nonviolence our way of life."[74] He argues that building peace "through active nonviolence is the natural and necessary complement to the Church's continuing efforts to limit the use of force by the application of moral norms."[75] This link between living in accord with dignity and active nonviolence is critical for re-imagined Catholic peacebuilding, and it seems to validate the argument about a possible shift from a just war tradition to a just peace approach.

Pope Francis seems to suggest that the Church will succeed more in its global peacebuilding role by prioritizing a just peace approach as "an effective way to transform conditions of violence and lead to just and sustainable peace."[76] The Just War principles (e.g., proportionality and discrimination) are good but appear more theoretical and idealistic. Experience has shown that, even with the best intention to uphold these principles during war, the killing and human suffering associated with war are hardly prevented, thereby justifying the saying that "realities are more important than ideas." In this case, the just peace approach considers real experiences of human and non-human creation and ethical realities in peacebuilding. It becomes the church's responsibility, as Eli McCarthy has argued, "to keep a just peace ethic front and center," because such an ethic enables the church to promote not only the inner disposition to "protect all life but even more so illuminate the sacred dignity of all persons and creation."[77] According to McCarthy, a "virtue-based just peace ethic" would make possible such a disposition and offer "norms which operate in three distinct, yet overlapping spheres" (*jus in conflictione, jus ex bello,* and *jus ad pacem*), with key virtues such as mercy, compassion, courage, justice, solidarity, empathy, hospitality, and active nonviolence, etc., to develop the "character necessary for the practices of a just peace ethic."[78] For McCarthy, a virtue-based just peace ethic enables the church "to transform conflict by addressing the personal, relational, structural, and cultural dimensions," and such an

---

/en/messages/pont-messages/2016/documents/papa-francesco_20160406_messaggio-non-violenza-pace-giusta.html.

[74] Pope Francis, "Nonviolence: A Style of Politics for Peace" (Message for World Day of Peace, January 1, 2017), no. 1, w2.vatican.va/content/francesco/en/messages/peace/documents/papa-francesco_20161208_messaggio-l-giornata-mondiale-pace-2017.html.

[75] Pope Francis, "Nonviolence: A Style of Politics for Peace," nos. 4 and 6.

[76] Lisa S. Cahill, *Blessed Are the Peacemakers: Pacifism, Just War, and Peacebuilding* (Minneapolis, MN: Fortress, 2019), vii.

[77] Eli S. McCarthy, "A Virtue-Based Just Peace Ethic," *Journal of Moral Theology* 7, no. 2 (2018): 100.

[78] McCarthy, "A Virtue-Based Just Peace Ethic," 95.

ethic "is more likely to actually prevent, limit, and move us toward outlawing war."[79] Based on Pope Francis's reference to the Sermon on the Mount as a "manual" for peacebuilding strategy,[80] McCarthy argues that the Pope strives towards a just peace ethic consistent with Jesus's teaching on nonviolent peacebuilding and he also challenges religious leaders to embrace such an ethic as disciples of Christ.[81] Francis himself argues that "to be true followers of Jesus today also includes embracing his teaching about nonviolence" and, as such, he pledges the "assistance of the Church in every effort to build peace through active and creative nonviolence."[82]

Pope Francis claims that an active and creative nonviolent peacebuilding approach can foster societal peace built on the values of justice, human dignity, human rights, and concern for the poor just as in PT and other continental and national peace documents discussed (EG, nos. 218–219). However, he envisions societal peace as a process under the framework of the CoE. That peacebuilding is a process neither means "returning to a time prior to conflicts," since "pain and conflict transform us," nor using "empty diplomacy, dissimulation, double-speak, hidden agendas, and good manners that mask reality" (FT, no. 226). It rather means that "every 'peace process requires enduring commitment [and] . . . is a patient effort to seek truth and justice, to honor the memory of victims and to open the way, step by step, to a shared hope stronger than the desire for vengeance'" (FT, no. 226). Such a process might appear to be time-wasting and frustrating but it is worth it, considering that time will always be greater than mere space. With these principles, Pope Francis indicates that constant commitment, active patience, truth, justice, and historical memory are vital to peacebuilding within the framework of the CoE.

Perhaps most importantly, there is a re-imagination of the notion of justice in the CoE peacebuilding paradigm. For Pope Francis, justice must be rooted in mercy, since the gospel of mercy inspires and guides the church to hear and respond to the cry for justice and its demands (EG, no. 188). Moreover, Pope Francis considers mercy as the "foundation of true justice" and the wellspring of peace.[83] From the perspective of peacebuilding, such justice seeks to repair broken relationships and harms caused by violent human actions, heal the victims, perpetrators, and community, transform the structures that

---

[79] McCarthy, "A Virtue-Based Just Peace Ethic," 100–101.
[80] Pope Francis, "Nonviolence: A Style of Politics for Peace," no. 6.
[81] McCarthy, "A Virtue-Based Just Peace Ethic," 93–94.
[82] Pope Francis, "Nonviolence: A Style of Politics for Peace," nos. 3 and 6.
[83] Pope Francis, *Misericordiae Vultus*, Bull of Indiction of the Extraordinary Jubilee of Mercy (April 11, 2015), nos. 21 and 2, w2.vatican.va/content/francesco/en/apost _letters/documents/papa-francesco_bolla_20150411_misericordiae-vultus.html.

perpetuate violence, and build sustainable peace. Hence, this justice is restorative. Francis argues that the notion of justice in peacebuilding processes "must integrate questions of justice in debates on the environment, so as to hear *both the cry of the earth and the cry of the poor*" (LS, no. 49, emphasis original), and ecological justice should be participatory and intergenerational (LS, no. 159). Thus, peacebuilding is "an ongoing process in which every new generation must take part" to achieve through a "multifaceted culture of encounter" (EG, no. 220). And where this is not the case, the church must raise its prophetic voice to forestall the spawning of new violence or conflicts in society (EG, no. 218).

Furthermore, there is an acknowledgment of the value of truth in the CoE peacebuilding paradigm just as in PT and CP respectively, but Francis reimagines truth by linking it to forgiveness and reconciliation as in the SECAM peace document. In the seventh chapter of *Fratelli Tutti* on the "Paths of Renewed Encounter," Pope Francis discusses "The Art and Architecture of Peace." He notes that "there is a need for paths of peace to heal open wounds" to renew human encounters in the world (FT, no. 225) and that such a renewed encounter requires the value of truth. Here, truth is fundamentally inseparable from the demands of justice and mercy, because the three values are not only essential but complement each other in any peacebuilding architecture (FT, no. 227). However, Pope Francis underscores the need to fulfill the demands of truth in a (violent) conflict situation, arguing that unveiling the truth in peacebuilding processes should aim at forgiveness and possible reconciliation rather than revenge (FT, no. 227). The act of revenge leads to a vicious cycle of violence and does not make for peacebuilding and renewed encounter (FT, no. 227), while the act of forgiveness and reconciliation presupposes the healing of "open wounds" (FT, no. 225). Laura Currie interprets the "open wound" to mean "a wounded memory that is in need of healing: that past or buried wounds and injustices have not, in fact, been resolved over time, as many would believe, and that this is a root cause of division contributing to today's social and political unrest."[84] For her, only when this historical memory has been healed can society move forward along the paths of forgiveness and reconciliation for renewed encounter and peacebuilding.[85]

For Pope Francis, "Reconciliation cannot simply entail a re-writing of history for the purpose of shifting blame."[86] It rather calls for

---

[84] Laura Currie, "Healing Memory: A Bonaventurian Response to Pope Francis's *Fratelli Tutti*," *Religions* 13, no. 819 (2022): 1.
[85] Currie, "Healing Memory," 2.
[86] Currie, "Healing Memory," 1.

"rapprochement between groups who took different sides at some troubled period of history" and "for a renewed encounter" in order "to recognize, protect, and concretely restore the dignity, so often overlooked or ignored, of our brothers and sisters, so that they can see themselves as the principal protagonists of the destiny of their nation" (FT, no. 233). One might posit that collaborative efforts to tackle the underlying causes of conflict (e.g., socioeconomic, political, and cultural) can facilitate a path towards mutual understanding and trust, both of which are pivotal in peacebuilding endeavors.

Pope Francis's CoE emphasizes social dialogue as a tool for peacebuilding processes. In his 2017 World Day of Peace message, he reaffirms PT's call to build peace on values of love, justice, truth, and freedom, and he passionately invites the church to participate in global "peacebuilding through active nonviolence" using dialogue as a tool.[87] Dialogue is a method of peacebuilding that has proven to be effective.[88] However, following American Mennonite and peace expert John Paul Lederach, such a dialogue process must ensure the inclusion and participation of every segment of society, able to build mutual trust, interrogate issues of justice at interpersonal and structural levels, and engender conversion and social transformation.[89] Hence it is social in nature. Here social dialogue uses the "elicitive method," in that it draws on local or cultural peacebuilding dialogue resources and allows dialogue parties to own the process and dialogue actions aimed at transforming conflicts and building sustainable peace.[90] As a peacebuilding mechanism or tool, social dialogue is necessary for assisting conflict actors to overcome bitter feelings and negative prejudices and biases against one another, considering that "it is no easy task to overcome the bitter legacy of injustices, hostility, and mistrust left by [a] conflict" (FT, no. 243).

Patient social dialogue and some form of negotiations underpinned by values of truth, justice, and mercy are capable of fostering reconciliation and building sustainable peace. Bringing these values to bear in social dialogue for peacebuilding forestalls peacebuilders from merely proclaiming "blanket reconciliation" which, at best, tends to gloss over the wounds and pain of those unjustly and cruelly treated, or to "cover injustices in a cloak of oblivion" simply because they happened in the past (FT, no. 246). Pope Francis decries the tendency to brush aside the past: "Nowadays it is easy to be tempted to turn the

---

[87] Pope Francis, "Nonviolence: A Style of Politics for Peace," nos. 5 and 6.
[88] Cahill, "The Changing Vision of 'Just Peace,'" 107–108.
[89] John Paul Lederach, *The Little Book of Conflict Transformation* (New York: Good Books, 2003), 21–22.
[90] John Paul Lederach, *Preparing for Peace: Conflict Transformation Across Cultures* (New York: Syracuse University Press, 1996), 55.

page, to say that all these things happened long ago, and we should look to the future. For God's sake, no! We can never move forward without remembering the past; we do not progress without an honest and unclouded memory" (FT, no. 249). So, building social peace requires social dialogue that uncovers past injustices, "rejects exclusion or manipulation," listens to all parties, and remains open to the truth and the pursuit of the good of human and non-human creation.[91]

As a tool for building sustainable social peace, social dialogue within Pope Francis's CoE envisions a holistic conception of peacebuilding. For Francis, building social peace—the "stability and security provided by a certain order which cannot be achieved without particular concern for distributive justice" (LS, no. 157)—is linked to inner personal peace which, in turn, "is closely related to care for ecology and for the common good" (LS, no. 225). Social peace is a "journey of ecological conversion" that must be understood integrally to stop "our hostility towards others, our lack of respect for our common home, or abusive exploitation of natural resources."[92] This is beautifully captured with Pope Francis's catchy phrase "integral ecology" (LS, nos. 137 and 225). Therefore, we understand social peace as one of the goals of the CoE, and such peace is built through a just peace approach. Social peace aims to maintain a healthy and balanced encounter (relationship) with God, oneself, others, and non-human creation, in keeping with God's established order.

This established order is creation itself, which Pope Francis refers to as "the order of love" (LS, no. 77), meaning that the whole of creation is ordered by God's love to be relational and interconnected. Building just peace on earth requires that humans observe diligently this order of interrelatedness and interconnectedness of all creation, respecting the "value proper to each creature" (LS, no. 16) since "every creature has its own value and significance" (LS, no. 76). Pope Francis goes beyond the acknowledgment of this divine order to offer CST the model of "integral ecology" as a moral framework for realizing the divinely established order of interconnectedness of all creation capable of fostering societal just peace. Integral ecology "represents an expanded moral vision" of building just peace not based on a technocratic paradigm but on a paradigm that links peacebuilding

---

[91] Pope Francis, "Peace as a Journey of Hope: Dialogue, Reconciliation, and Ecological Conversion" (Message for World Day of Peace, January 1, 2020), no. 2, w2.vatican.va/content/francesco/en/messages/peace/documents/papa-francesco_20191208_messaggio-53giornatamondiale-pace2020.html.
[92] Pope Francis, "Peace as a Journey," no. 4.

to issues of justice (at the social, economic, and political levels), ecological or environmental concerns, sustainable development, etc.[93]

Based on the framework of the CoE, holistic Catholic peacebuilding would be an integral ecology model that recognizes the intrinsic value of all creation (human and non-human) rather than treating them "as parts that can be utilized and profited from, consumed or used to varying degrees, and then disposed of."[94] This peacebuilding model "suggests the need for a new consideration of the idea of just peace, one that explicitly involves ecological sustainability and restorative justice for the planet."[95] The guiding principles for this new consideration are respect for human and non-human creation and restoration of relationships between human beings and God, among human beings, and between human beings and creation.[96] Experience has shown that social conflict and violence have ensued in most places where proper attention was not given to this new consideration.[97] A typical case is Nigeria's Niger Delta violent conflict. Hence, we return to the question of how Pope Francis's CoE peacebuilding framework can assist the Nigerian Catholic Church in building sustainable peace in the Niger Delta region.

IMPLICATIONS FOR RETHINKING THE NIGERIAN CATHOLIC CHURCH'S PEACEBUILDING STRATEGIES

Although a few successes have been recorded, the Nigerian Catholic Church's peacebuilding strategies have not been able to transform and build lasting peace in the Niger Delta region. As mentioned earlier, the region still suffers intermittent physical violence, and the socioeconomic and political structures that precipitated the violence in the first place have yet to be transformed. In light of the CoE peacebuilding model, the Nigerian Catholic Church can contribute to the transformation of these unjust structures and thus end the structural and physical violence in the region by going beyond the strategies of merely issuing statements and engaging in charitable activities, and beginning to actually build a sustainable and dynamic social peace in the region. Although the church's strategies have

---

[93] Anna F. Scheid and Daniel P. Scheid, "Integral Ecology, Just Peace, and Mining," in Caesar A. Montevecchio and Gerard F. Powers, eds., *Catholic Peacebuilding and Mining: Integral Peace, Development, and Ecology* (New York: Routledge, 2022), 120.
[94] Scheid and Scheid, "Integral Ecology," 130.
[95] Scheid and Scheid, "Integral Ecology," 122.
[96] Scheid and Scheid, "Integral Ecology," 124–126.
[97] Jessica L. Imanaka, Greg Prussia, and Samantha Alexis, "*Laudato Si'* and Integral Ecology: A Reconceptualization of Sustainability," *Journal of Management for Global Sustainability* 5, no. 1 (2017): 39–61.

identified injustice as the root cause of the violence and have called for remediation of justice in the region as well as conversion and dialogue by conflict actors, there has been a lack of active involvement and participation on the part of the church towards realizing this call. There has been no peace advocacy program or collaboration with local and international peace advocacy groups, no dialogue or interface with the Nigerian government and MNCs to discuss issues of structural injustice raised in the communiqués regarding the violence, no deployment of media to publicize these issues and thus internationalize the violence, and no emphasis on local/cultural peace resources in peacebuilding processes in the region. The absence of these elements in the church's peacebuilding intervention strategies in the Niger Delta reveals an obvious pitfall that necessitates a rethinking of the strategies in light of the CoE peacebuilding model. Hence, the following suggestions.

First, the church has to become credible and trustworthy in a society like Nigeria where there is a growing suspicion and accusation of the church's hierarchy aligning with the political elite that cares not so much about the unjust and poor condition of the Niger Deltans and their environment. This credibility can come through renewed self-identity and prophetic witness, whereby the church's structures embody certain values such as mercy, compassion, poverty, humility, truth, impartiality, justice, freedom, and dialogical discernment. The church's documents on the Niger Delta conflict need to be more critical and transparently clear on its stance regarding burning issues in the region, such as the protection of and respect for human life and dignity, human rights, and creation, by tasking the government and MNCs to provide basic and social amenities and safeguard the environment. Also, the church has to exhibit courageous patience in the pursuit of peacebuilding and the common good in the region. With all this, the church can explicitly renounce the accusation of alignment and gain the trust of the Niger Delta people and the conflict actors.

Second, with its earned credibility and trust, the Nigerian Church can collaborate with other religious bodies if necessary to initiate and facilitate a peacebuilding dialogue process among the conflict actors. It is not enough for the church, both as individuals and institution, to call the conflicting parties to toe the path of dialogue.[98] The church must be involved in actualizing the call. In facilitating such a dialogue

---

[98] CBCN, Communiqué "We Must Pull Back from the Brink of Collapse" (Orlu: February 23, 2021), no. 8, w2.nigeriacatholicnetwork.com/cbcn-communique-february-2021/; Jude Atemanke, "Nigerian Archbishop Advocates for Dialogue, Says 'Peace is Never Achieved on Battlefield,'" *Association for Catholic Information in Africa* (May 16, 2022), w2.aciafrica.org/news/5854/nigerian-archbishop-advocates-for-dialogue-says-peace-is-never-achieved-on-battlefield.

process, the church can draw insights from the CoE peacebuilding model and the Colombian community-based pastoral dialogue approach, which involves empathic listening and accompaniment of the various militant groups to foster forgiveness, justice, reconciliation, and peace. The church can also ask its organs, such as the Justice, Development, and Peace Commission (JDPC) and Catholic Caritas Foundation of Nigeria (CCFN) to initiate and facilitate the peacebuilding dialogue.

For example, CCFN, in collaboration with the State Peace Commission in Kaduna and Plateau (both are states in Nigeria), facilitated a peacebuilding dialogue process (from February 1, 2021, to March 31, 2022) with state representatives from academia, religious groups, community leaders, youth groups, women groups, government, artists, CSOs, and the media. The process began with the mapping of the violent conflict by listening to the stories of the different parties involved in the conflict (e.g., Plateau: selected leaders on the ground—male elders, women, youths, politicians, and academics—adjudged to have good reputations both from the Fulanis and the Plateau people) to underscore what is at stake. Although the states are not completely free from violent conflict, the dialogue process has restored relative peace and led to increased intercultural and interreligious tolerance in both states. The dialogue process also initiated mid-term and long-term initiatives, such as interreligious activities (women peace dialogue forum, youth peace dialogue forum, interreligious radio peace programs in local languages, etc.) that promote intercultural and religious pluralism, scholarship grants to students in the field of conflict transformation and peacebuilding, sponsoring artists to entertain community and state peace matches and gatherings, training of media personnel and journalists, sponsoring interreligious conferences and public cultural events, etc.[99]

Another example is the *Zaman Tare* (Living Together), a peace dialogue process gradually transforming a violent conflict and building sustainable peace in Nigeria's Kaduna and Plateau states. The peacebuilding dialogue process, funded by the European Union, was facilitated by the Nigerian Catholic Church through CCFN and coordinated by the Catholic Agency for Overseas Development (CAFOD). In addition to Borno State (the birth state of Boko Haram), Plateau and Kaduna states have been a hotbed of intractable violent conflicts, which some scholars have identified as either ethno-religious, political, resource-based, inter-communal, herder-farmer, or identity conflict, with thousands of human lives lost.[100]

---

[99] CCFN, "Final Report on *Zaman Tare* (Living Together): Intercultural Dialogue and Culture Project" (Abuja: Catholic Secretariat of Nigeria, 2023).

[100] See Solomon Anjide and Obinna C. Amaechi, "The Intractability of Violent Conflict in Nigeria: A Study of Plateau State," *GOUNI Journal of Management and*

The church can, like the above examples in which it initiated and facilitated peacebuilding dialogue in states of Nigeria's northern region, extend such a dialogue process to the Niger Delta region. However, it has to take into consideration the specificity of the region and the violent conflict itself while drawing on insights from peacebuilding principles as framed in the CoE peacebuilding model. To do so will entail that the peacebuilding dialogue process must be open to truth and willing to engage the unjust social, economic, political, and ecological realities that underlie the violent conflict in the region. With such openness, the process might transcend mere ideas to facilitate dialogue aimed at resolving these practical realities through concerted efforts toward promoting justice, mercy, forgiveness, attitudinal conversion, and peaceful reconciliation among the parties. Also, facilitating a dialogue process to transform the complexities of the root causes of the Niger Delta violent conflict and build lasting peace would certainly take much time and require the virtue of patience on the part of the church. It would also require "multiple social levels and a wide time horizon that involves healing the past as well as envisioning the future, and an 'elicitive' method that taps local cultures for their peacebuilding codes."[101] In facilitating the peacebuilding dialogue process, the church must represent the needs[102] of the conflict parties while bearing in mind the sufferings of the people of the Niger Delta.[103] As such, I recommend the following steps for the dialogue process:

- Framing the conflict by listening to the stories of all the conflict parties to properly identify the nature, socioeconomic, political, and environmental root causes, and dynamics of the conflict. This aims to make room for different ways of understanding the conflict and thus appreciate the people's diverse possibilities and contributions towards transforming the conflict and building

---

Social Sciences 10, no. 1 (2022): 215–228; Shittu Aro, "Analysis of the Nature of Violence in Kaduna, Nigeria," *Applied Research Journal of Science and Technology* 3, no. 1 (2022):1–15.

[101] Daniel Philpott, "Introduction: Searching for Strategy in an Age of Peacebuilding," in Daniel Philpott and Gerard F. Powers, eds., *Strategies of Peace: Transforming Conflict in a Violent World* (New York: Oxford University Press, 2010), 11.

[102] The practice of identifying the element of needs of conflict actors by dialogue facilitators is crucial for an effective peacebuilding dialogue process, hence the need to train facilitators in nonviolent communication that espouses and valorizes this element alongside other elements such as centering, observations, feelings, and requests (see "What is Nonviolent Communication?," w2.cnvc.org/learn/what-is-nvc#!/p/471389513).

[103] David Kwon, "*Jus Post Bellum* and Catholic Social Thought: Just Political Participation as Civil Society Peacebuilding," *Journal of Catholic Social Thought* 20, no. 2 (2023): 424.

sustainable peace. While this analysis is going on, the church can identify with the struggles, cries, and pains of the victims of the conflict through pastoral accompaniment and charity.

- Seeking new opportunities by being morally imaginative to envision new and creative ways, such as conscience formation, peacebuilding education, and advocacy, to make all the parties accountable and responsible; ensuring that their extractive activities do not violate human dignity, human rights, and environmental rights, thereby making way for sustainable peacebuilding. Here, I suggest organizing peacebuilding seminars and symposia for all parties in a safe space.

- Ensuring that the dialogue process taps and mobilizes available local peacebuilding resources that take into account the socio-cultural and spiritual worldviews of the Nigerian/Niger Delta context.

- Adopting a participatory and inclusive dialogical process that is bottom-up in approach, thereby ensuring that agency is given to the people, knowing that "everyone has a fundamental role to play in a single great creative project" of peacebuilding and reconciliation.[104] This bottom-up approach will equip the different conflicting actors to "take ownership of their lives and to assume responsibility through their daily commitments to bringing about" a peaceful and environmentally flourishing Niger Delta region.[105]

A third element is advocacy and internationalization. Peace-building advocacy focuses more on changing unjust structures that trigger violent conflicts and on human rights violations within a violent conflict setting. The Niger Delta violent conflict has underlying unjust socioeconomic, political, and environmental structures as root causes and cases of human dignity and human rights violations. Hence, there is a need for the Nigerian Church to engage in peacebuilding advocacy. Furthermore, the violent conflict involves the Nigerian state and MNCs on one side and the people of the Niger Delta on the other, suggesting the presence of underlying power differentials. In such a context, advocacy initiatives (e.g., nonviolent marches or protests, mass petitions, public declarations, boycotts, civil resistance, etc.)[106] could enhance the effectiveness of the peace-building

---

[104] Pope Francis, "Interreligious Meeting with Youth in Maputo, Mozambique," *L'Osservatore Romano* (6 September 2019): 7.
[105] Francis, "Interreligious Meeting."
[106] See Veronique Dudouet, "Powering to Peace: Integrated Civil Resistance and Peacebuilding Strategies," *International Center on Nonviolent Conflict Special*

dialogue process. Such advocacy initiatives might require that the church's agencies, such as the Catholic Caritas Foundation of Nigeria (CCFN), Justice, Development, and Peace Commission (JDPC), etc., collaborate with other local faith-based peace advocacy groups and secular Civil Society Organizations (CSOs) to organize nonviolent peace initiatives (e.g., a peace march). Similarly, the church through CCFN and JDPC, can collaborate with the Traditional Rulers Council (TRC) in all the states of the Niger Delta region to demand good governance and fiscal accountability and zero corruption from all stakeholders. That way, corruption, one of the reasons for the intractability of the violent conflict in the region, will be nipped in the bud. The overarching goal of engaging in advocacy initiatives/ programs is to draw the attention of conflict actors to the deleterious effects of the violent conflict and mobilize the Niger Delta population to nonviolently resist unjust structures and extractive policies and practices by the Nigerian government and MNCs respectively.

Moreover, because the violent conflict involves the Nigerian state and MNCs there is a need for the church to engage local and international CSOs, as well as the help of international Catholic and non-Catholic peace advocacy groups. For example, the church can engage the services of Sant' Egidio which negotiated peacebuilding dialogue in Mozambique, and Catholic Relief Services which advocates for peace in sub-Sahara Africa and other regions of the world torn apart by resource-based violent conflicts. Internationalization of the Niger Delta violent conflict via engagement of international advocacy groups is necessary considering that the violent conflict somehow affects the rest of the world because of the reality of interconnectedness. Collaborating with international advocacy groups appears beneficial because such organizations might help to exert legitimate pressure on international forces (e.g., crude oil syndicates, arms dealers, etc.) whose merchandise benefits immensely from the violent conflict. It will also exert legitimate pressure on both the Nigerian government and MNCs to change unjust structures that marginalize and exclude the people of the region, as well as foster change in extractive laws and policies that impoverish the people and damage their environment.

Finally, the church can also engage the Nigerian government in the areas of policymaking and implementation, especially policies relating to oil and gas activity. It could realize this by permitting JDPC, in collaboration with local and international civil groups, to oversee a platform for reflections on good governance and ethical mining of natural resources. JDPC will, in turn, advise the church on

---

Report Series, no. 1 (April 2017), www.academia.edu/34730320/Powering_to_Peace _Integrated_Civil_Resistance_and_Peacebuilding_Strategies.

policies and laws related to the extraction and management of natural resources. With that, the church can engage the government in policymaking and implementation in the field of oil and gas extraction. This strategy worked for the bishops' Conference of the Democratic Republic of Congo (CENCO). CENCO created the Episcopal Commission for Natural Resources (CERN) which, in turn, advised the bishops on all conflicts related to the exploitation of natural resources in DRC. Armed with the advice of CERN, the church in DRC was able to engage and influence the DRC government in policymaking.[107]

CONCLUSION

Building social peace has become a constitutive dimension of the church's evangelizing mission, with its conception and ways of achieving global peace reimagined under Francis's papacy that has the culture of encounter as a defining mark. The culture of encounter calls for ecclesial and missionary as well as ecological conversion; as such, the CoE engenders the process of renewed ecclesial self-identity and prophetic witnessing. With this new self-identity and prophetic witness, the CoE refocuses the church's social mission, such as conflict transformation and peacebuilding via four ethical principles capable of enhancing virtues for political life such as responsible citizenship, participation, truth, mercy, the common good, and justice. These virtues take on board the protection of human dignity and human rights without neglecting genuine concern for the poor and form the basis on which social peace is built in any society using a just peace approach. As a result, Pope Francis has relentlessly promoted these virtues for peacebuilding through his writings and symbolic actions from the beginning of his pontificate. This indicates that Pope Francis's global peacebuilding agenda, as evidenced by his call for the promotion of a culture of encounter, pleads for a more practical and exemplary demonstration of the art of peacebuilding that takes an active nonviolent approach seriously.

Francis has pursued the global peace agenda of the church not just through words but also deeds. Although Francis has no major document that exclusively deals with the theme of peacebuilding, some of the pope's encyclicals, apostolic exhortations, addresses, messages, and homilies refer to peacebuilding. Pope Francis has engaged in international apostolic and diplomatic visits intentionally aimed at promoting global peace, such as the visit to the cities of

---

[107] See Rigobert Minani, "The Mining Industry, Conflict, and the Church's Commitment in the Democratic Republic of the Congo," in *Catholic Peacebuilding and Mining*, 45–53.

Hiroshima and Nagasaki in Japan (2019), the Central African Republic (2015), Egypt (2017), Cuba (2015), Colombia (2017), United Arab Emirates (2019), South Sudan and DRC (2023), etc. Apart from these visits, Pope Francis has also demonstrated peacebuilding gestures such as hosting a day of prayer for Mahmoud Abbas (Palestinian president) and Shimon Peres (then Israeli president) at the Vatican in 2014, signing the joint document on "Human Fraternity for World Peace and Living Together" with Ahmad Al-Tayyeb (Grand Imam of Al-Azhar) on February 4, 2019, organizing a retreat for Muslim and Christian political leaders of South Sudan at the Vatican in 2019, etc. At the heart of these peacebuilding initiatives and gestures is, for Thomas Massaro, the notion of the CoE that defines Francis's papacy.[108]

Pope Francis believes that the synergy of the church and people of goodwill can create "a special place of encounter . . . where believers and non-believers are able to engage in dialogue about fundamental issues" such as global peacebuilding (EG, no. 257). That is what the culture of encounter aims at: the coming together of all people from diverse social, religious, academic, and other fields of life to work for a peaceful society where human and non-human creation will flourish. For him, a complete conception of peacebuilding pursues a peaceful relationship with our maker, one another, and non-human creation, "since everything is interrelated" (LS, no. 120). To construct such a peacebuilding architecture, we need to engage in social dialogue open to the truth while vigorously but non-violently seeking to protect human dignity and human rights, promote social, economic, political, and ecological justice, and preferential care for the poor, the unjustly excluded, and those pushed to fringes of society. Francis summarizes his CoE peacebuilding model with what he calls "integral ecology," and he invites all to experience ecological conversion.

Through the practice of the CoE within and outside of itself, the Catholic Church might experience a conversion for renewed self-identity and prophetic witness and become more effective in its social mission, such as promoting global peacebuilding using social dialogue as a tool and active nonviolence as an approach. This applies to particular churches such as the Nigerian Catholic Church, for it can also experience similar conversion by practicing a culture of encounter. With renewed self-identity and prophetic witness as fruits of conversion, the Nigerian Catholic Church can rethink its peacebuilding strategies in the Niger Delta region in light of the CoE peacebuilding model. The church could become more credible and trustworthy before the conflict actors to facilitate the peacebuilding

---

[108] Thomas Massaro, "The Peace Advocacy of Pope Francis: Jesuit Perspectives," *Journal of Jesuit Studies* 8 (2021): 536–543.

social dialogue process in the region. Such a dialogue process would creatively frame the conflict and seek new opportunities for collaboration; tap into and incorporate local peacebuilding resources; and adopt an inclusive, participatory, and bottom-up approach. Furthermore, the church needs to engage in peace advocacy programs and collaborate with local and international advocacy groups, adopt proper use of media communication, and engage in state-church collaboration in extractive policymaking. That way, it can contribute to transforming the natural resource-based conflict and building sustainable peace in the region for the flourishing of the Niger Deltans and their environment, the Nigerian state, and the MNCs operating in the region. M

Martin Owhorchukwu Ejiowhor, a Nigerian and Catholic priest of the Diocese of Port Harcourt, Nigeria is a doctoral student at the Catholic University of Leuven, Belgium, and belongs to the Theological and Comparative Ethics Research Unit. His areas of research are the dynamics of justice and love, the notion of the culture of encounter, social dialogue, religious peacebuilding, and social transformation.

Theologizing Across Psychology: Experiences of Depression, Trauma, and Moral Injury

Stephanie C. Edwards and Catherine Yanko

THE FOLLOWING ARTICLES BY STEPHANIE C. EDWARDS and Catherine Yanko expand upon research originally presented at the 2024 College Theology Society (CTS) conference in Denver, Colorado in the context of a panel titled: "Hearing and Healing Psychological Hurt: Trauma, Moral Injury, and *Dust in the Blood* (CTS 2023 Best Book)." Their work constituted a panel engaging Jessica Coblentz's book, *Dust in the Blood: A Theology of Life with Depression* (Liturgical Press Academic, 2022). Both authors present arguments shaped by Coblentz's methodology and her assessment of theology's intersection with depression. Yanko's 5and Edwards's articles model a book discussion where the respondents, as such, offer research developments inspired and informed by the author, rather than presenting a more traditional direct critique of the work itself. Their engagements are followed by Coblentz's own response to their expansions of her research.

First, Yanko extends Coblentz's impulse to narrative and phenomenology by applying the theological framework presented in *Dust in the Blood* to the experience of moral injury. Coblentz's inductive and highly contextualized theology inspires Yanko to study conscience through the experience of moral injury. Yanko argues that these insights about conscience can aid theologians in overcoming points of impasse in contemporary debates about conscience in Catholic moral theology. Second, Edwards engages Coblentz's concept of "wilderness" through her work in trauma. Following an initial assessment of the connections between depression (as read by Coblentz) and trauma studies, Edwards moves into ethical construction. Viewing mental health disorders as alive in the social realm, as well as distinctly individual, Edwards offers a Christian social ethic she names "enfleshed counter-memory." Cobletnz responds to both authors.

Both Edwards and Yanko utilize Coblentz as foundational to their own research and theological "next steps." When read together, the authors intend to inspire scholars to rethink their own work through Coblentz's lens, recognizing the tendrils of issues such as mental health, disability, and embodiment that entwine themselves in every facet of theology. The trio of papers is intended to represent one iteration of an ongoing conversation in theology regarding anthropology, mental health, and ethics. M

Investigating Moral Injury: Thinking Beyond the Law-Conscience Binary

Catherine Yanko

Abstract: In *Dust in the Blood*, Jessica Coblentz notes the insufficiency of theodical approaches to theology to account for depressive suffering. Instead, she proposes a theology of depression that makes use of narrative-phenomenological portraits and draws new insights on what Christian discipleship means in the context of depressive suffering. In this article, I employ Coblentz's framework to interrogate another area of contemporary theology. Debates about the moral authority of conscience are largely unresolved. In order to confront some points of intractable disagreement in these debates and consider a way beyond them, I study firsthand experiences of moral injury. Jonathon Shay, the clinical psychiatrist who coined the term, defined moral injury as "a betrayal of what's right by someone who holds legitimate authority in a high stakes situation." From patterns in firsthand experiences of moral injury, I propose a respective understanding of conscience. I argue that this understanding of conscience can direct theologians beyond impasses in Catholic moral theology.

IN THEIR ARTICLE, "BEYOND THE LAW AND CONSCIENCE BINARY in Catholic Moral Thought," David Cloutier and Robert Koerpel described contemporary moral theology as at an impasse. This is most plainly exhibited in intractable disagreements over divorce and remarriage about *Amoris Laetitia*. Cloutier and Koerpel traced the impasse to what they term the "law-conscience binary." Today, law and conscience are defined in opposition to each other: conscience is proposed as a corrective alternative to law and vice versa.[1] This forms a binary: defining law and conscience in this way makes law and conscience "the site of conflict between two different wills, where each will competes with the other's notion of moral authority."[2]

As long as this binary persists in Catholic moral theology, resolution in debates like the one surrounding *Amoris Laetitia* is difficult to imagine. To think beyond the law-conscience binary, I will employ what Jessica Coblentz called "narrative phenomenological

---

[1] David Cloutier and Robert Koerpel, "Beyond the Law-Conscience Binary in Catholic Moral Thought," *Journal of Moral Theology* 10, no. 2 (2021): 176.
[2] Cloutier and Koerpel, "Beyond the Law-Conscience Binary," 177.

portraits." In *Dust in the Blood*, Coblentz developed a theology of depression grounded in narrative phenomenological portraits.[3] By considering the way conscience is described in narrative phenomenological portraits of moral injury, I argue that the insight gained into conscience can aid moral theologians today to think beyond the law-conscience binary.

THEOLOGY AND DEPRESSION: NARRATIVE-PHENOMENOLOGICAL PORTRAITS

Noting the prevalence of depression and its increasing rate, Coblentz recounted her surprise at discovering the lacunae of theological resources discussing depression.[4] To address these lacunae, Coblentz described how she first turned to various studies of suffering in Christian theology. These studies, dominated by "rational proofs, theodical explanations, and intellectual apologies," primarily focused on justifying the existence of suffering in view of a good God.[5] Noting how these studies have "explain[ed] away the grave horrors of history," Coblentz asserted these ways of studying suffering as insufficient.[6] As an alternative, Coblentz turned to theologians who understood the need to give an account of these horrors: Johann Baptist Metz, Dorothee Sölle, and Edward Schillebeeckx. These theologians address suffering through narrative theological approaches. According to Coblentz, these approaches "uphold the particularities of suffering, including its contradictions and fragmentations."[7] This is to say, where some approaches to theologies of suffering depersonalize and disembody those suffering, narrative theological approaches account for the experience of suffering in its context and complexities.[8]

---

[3] Coblentz has extended this way of doing theology beyond *Dust in the Blood*. The following articles by Coblentz both explore and rely on this inductive way of doing theology and/or further investigate the relationship between theology, ethics, mental health, and psychology: "What Can Theology Offer Psychology? Some Considerations in the Context of Depression?," *Journal of Moral Theology* 9, no. 1 (2020): 2–19; "I. Theological Reflection on White Women's Misery," *Horizons* 50, no. 1 (2023): 180–190, doi.org/10.1017/hor.2023.6; "The Possibilities of Grace amid Persistent Depression," *Theological Studies* 80, no. 3 (2019): 554–571, doi.org/10.1177/004056 3919857184; "Ghosts in the Office: The Ecclesiological and Soteriological Implications of Stereotype Threat among Women in Catholic Theology," *Journal of Feminist Studies in Religion* 33, no. 1 (2017): 127–135, doi.org/10.2979/jfemistudreli.33.1.11.
[4] Jessica Coblentz, *Dust in the Blood: A Theology of Life with Depression* (Collegeville, MN: Liturgical Press Academic, 2022), 6–7.
[5] Coblentz, *Dust in the Blood*, 7.
[6] Coblentz, *Dust in the Blood*, 7–8.
[7] Coblentz, *Dust in the Blood*, 8.
[8] Coblentz, *Dust in the Blood*, 10–11.

In her own theological approach, Coblentz accounts for this personal dimension by reflecting on firsthand experiences. Here, she is motivated by the "epistemological gains" made by liberation and political theologians like Ada María Isasi-Díaz.[9] Isasi-Díaz's *mujerista* theology reflected on the everyday experience of Latina women. The knowledge gained through reflection on these experiences informs how Isasi-Díaz and other *mujerista* theologians understand God and the world. According to Coblentz, firsthand experiences provide insight into dimensions of an experience that those who have not shared these experiences would not be "inclined to apprehend."[10] By taking a narrative theological approach that prioritizes firsthand accounts of depression, Coblentz's resulting theology of depression accounts for the personal and embodied dimensions of human experience.

To organize the first-person accounts of depression presented in the first chapter for theological study, Coblentz discerned patterns. The pattern that Coblentz noticed, which grounded her subsequent theology of depression, was an experience of unhomelikeness. She arrived at this description by subjecting first-person accounts of depression to phenomenological analysis.[11] Following Husserlian phenomenologists, Coblentz attended to the subjective experience of self as a lived-body (*Leib*). To do this, she bracketed any causal frameworks through which an experience would be described (e.g., genetic make-up or proper nutrients). Then, she studied the lifeworld (*Lebenswelt*) of the subject, or the world as it presents itself to the subject.[12] This method allows phenomenologists to be attentive to different moods (*Stimmungen*). Mood here refers to what grounds or pre-conditions the way a subject experiences the world. Drawing from Heideggerian phenomenology, Coblentz argued that depression is a shift in mood (*Stimmung*): it shifts in a pre-thematic way how someone interacts with the world.[13] In contrast to a mood of "at-home-ness" (*Heimlichkeit*) and experiences of connection and shared belonging, unhomelikeness (*Unheimlichkeit*) brings a denuding of meaning and loss of bodily resonance with the world.[14]

According to Coblentz, the phenomenological understanding of the state of unhomelikeness resonates with the patterns that emerge from first-person accounts of depression. For example, like unhomelikeness, depression leaves people with an absence of familiarity in

---

[9] Coblentz, *Dust in the Blood*, 9.
[10] Coblentz, *Dust in the Blood*, 9.
[11] Coblentz, *Dust in the Blood*, 35.
[12] Coblentz, *Dust in the Blood*, 35.
[13] Coblentz, *Dust in the Blood*, 38.
[14] Coblentz, *Dust in the Blood*, 39–40.

their everyday lives. Unhomelikeness also resonates with the experience of radical isolation by those who suffer from depression. Depression, like unhomelikeness, resists meaningfulness. Additionally, unhomelikeness accounts for the feeling of permanence and helpless entrapment those who suffer from depression experience.[15] Coblentz deemed this description of depression as unhomelikeness a much richer foundation for a theology of depression.

In *Dust in the Blood*, Coblentz then proceeded to draw theological insights and conclusions by relating depression under the description of unhomelikeness to the Scriptures. First, Coblentz considered the story of Hagar. Unlike popular theories surveyed in the second chapter that rely on understanding depression as a moral evil and theodical approaches that premise a distant and uninvolved God, this story reveals God as the one who "sees and hears."[16] Describing Hagar's story, Coblentz said, "Her suffering remains illogical, and God is nevertheless working and present in their midst."[17] Hagar's experience of her own suffering and relation to God become paradigmatic in Coblentz's theology of depression. Faith prompts the person suffering from depression not to necessarily find an answer for why suffering is happening but to discover the radical presence of God.[18] From this, Coblentz concluded to new possibilities for understanding salvation in the context of the wilderness of depressive suffering: "to hope against hope—to *hope that* salvation will come even when they cannot possibly perceive *what* salvation will look like."[19]

Coblentz's proposal of what salvation means in the context of the suffering of depression has implications for Christian discipleship. As disciples, Christians seek to imitate God as their teacher.[20] In Coblentz's theology, where God is understood as the one who sees and hears, Christian discipleship thus entails things like unimposing accompaniment,[21] social transformation—and even revolution—of the injustices that sometimes enable depression,[22] providing access to mental health resources,[23] and overcoming stigmatization.[24] To do this, it is imperative that Christians cultivate a narrative that encourages Christians to "stay with" their unresolved suffering like Hagar and lean into the inability to reconcile divine benevolence with

---

[15] Coblentz, *Dust in the Blood*, 41–42.
[16] Coblentz, *Dust in the Blood*, 175.
[17] Coblentz, *Dust in the Blood*, 176.
[18] Coblentz, *Dust in the Blood*, 177–178.
[19] Coblentz, *Dust in the Blood*, 194.
[20] Coblentz, *Dust in the Blood*, 200.
[21] Coblentz, *Dust in the Blood*, 201–203.
[22] Coblentz, *Dust in the Blood*, 208.
[23] Coblentz, *Dust in the Blood*, 209.
[24] Coblentz, *Dust in the Blood*, 213.

the horrors of suffering.[25] Emerging out of her theology of depression, Coblentz proposed a distinct definition of salvation that rivals salvation construed in theodical approaches that seek to reconcile God's goodness and the evils of suffering: "salvation consists not in resolving suffering through the assertion of quick theological fixes but rather in supporting possibilities for survival and quality of life through offerings of theological, social, and material resources."[26]

By studying firsthand accounts of depression and subjecting them to phenomenological inquiry, Coblentz proposed a definition of salvation that overcomes many shortcomings faced by theodical approaches. Her definition honors the subjectivity of the human person rather than flattens or minimizes the experience of suffering by "withhold[ing] the imposition of meaning and divine justifications."[27] She is also able to account for the unique wisdom gained by those who suffer from depression. Through an impact on mood, those who suffer from depression have a unique lifeworld experience. Being shaped by unhomelikeness, those who suffer from depression can gain insight that others may have a difficult time grasping. According to Coblentz, those who suffer from depression are uniquely posed to understand the salvific character of hoping in the wilderness.[28] In the proceeding sections, I will apply Coblentz's method to the experience of moral injury. By studying moral injury in this way, I argue that the unique insights into conscience gained can aid theologians who want to think beyond the law-conscience binary.

A PORTRAIT OF MORAL INJURY

Today, moral injury is used to refer to a variety of situations whereby someone experiences "moral fracturing."[29] Richardson, Lamson, and Hutto use the term "moral fracturing" to describe the experience veterans/former service members who have experienced moral injury commonly have of one's "whole moral base and moral

---

[25] Coblentz, *Dust in the Blood*, 208–209.
[26] Coblentz, *Dust in the Blood*, 217.
[27] Coblentz, *Dust in the Blood*, 217.
[28] Coblentz, *Dust in the Blood*, 194.
[29] Natalie M. Richardson, Angela L. Lamson, and Olivia Hutto, "'My Whole Base and Moral Understanding Was Shattered': A Phenomenological Understanding of Key Definitional Constructs of Moral Injury," *Traumatology* 28, no. 4 (2022): 463, 466–467, doi.org/10.1037/trm0000364. In this article, the authors conduct a study on firsthand experiences of moral injury. They found that the self-description of "fracturing" or "shattering" is highly common amongst participants. Throughout this article, I will refer to this first-person description of moral injury. Grounding the argument on first-person accounts allows it to be an exercise in Coblentz's method of reflecting in firsthand experiences to gain theological insight.

understanding [being] shattered."[30] This phenomenon is accompanied by guilt, demoralization, and isolation. In working with veterans/ former service members, Richardson, Lamson, and Hutto found that this fracturing is the result of a choice that contradicts what the human person believed to be good in a high stakes situation. The choice executed in these situations would be considered undesirable and uncharacteristic by her if she was not facing some constraint. Typically, this context involves some authority that demands, coerces, or strongly encourages the choice executed.[31]

The term "moral injury" was coined in the context of therapeutic interventions for veterans returning from the Vietnam War. Working at the Veteran Affairs (VA) Boston Outpatient Clinic, a long-term outpatient program for combat veterans, Jonathan Shay, a clinical psychiatrist, identified common experiences among his clients. He noticed many similarities between the veterans' experiences and the Homeric characters' experience in the *Iliad*—particularly in the experience of "betrayal of what's right by a commander and the onset of the berserk state."[32] Through their work in clinical contexts, Shay and Munroe argued that the veterans' postwar experience is centered around the betrayal they experienced in war. These authors noted that many of their clients trace their present suffering to the exploitation and betrayal they experienced by those who held credentials over them and responsibility for their well-being during the war.[33]

In their chapter in *Posttraumatic Stress Disorder: A Comprehensive Text*, Shay and Munroe used the term "moral injury" to describe this experience of betrayal commonly felt by veterans.[34] While "moral injury" was initially used in a passing way, not intended as a novel point of development in clinical research, it quickly attracted attention because of its ability to name key components of veterans' common experiences.[35] Informed by their clinical practice, Shay and Munroe further developed the idea of moral injury and propose the following three-part definition: "1) a betrayal of what's right; 2) by someone

---

[30] Richardson, Lamson, and Hutto, "'My Whole Base and Moral Understanding,'" 466.
[31] Richardson, Lamson, and Hutto, "'My Whole Base and Moral Understanding,'" 463–467.
[32] Jonathan Shay, *Achilles in Vietnam: Combat Trauma and the Undoing of Character* (New York: Simon & Schuster, 1994), xiii.
[33] Jonathan Shay and James Munroe, "Group and Milieu Therapy for Veterans with Complex Posttraumatic Stress Disorder," in *Posttraumatic Stress Disorder: A Comprehensive Text*, ed. Phillip A. Saigh and J. Douglas Bremner (Needham Heights, MA: Allyn & Bacon, 1999), 392.
[34] Shay and Munroe, "Group and Milieu Therapy for Veterans," 391–392.
[35] Jonathan Shay, "Moral Injury," *Psychoanalytic Psychology* 31, no. 2 (2014): 183, doi.org/10.1037/a0036090.

who holds legitimate authority; 3) in a high stakes situation."[36] In Shay's understanding of the concept, moral injury primarily relates to a political wound: it is something inflicted in relation to others.[37]

In the Vietnam War, Shay argued that moral injury occurred when subordinates executed the command of their superiors even though it was contrary to what the subordinates considered to be the moral decision. A sense of betrayal was commonly felt after due to the experience of seeing that the choice made was the best or only option and subsequent feelings of intense guilt and shame. Similar to how Homer describes in the *Iliad*, the experiences of Vietnam veterans show that moral injury impacts people in a lasting way—well beyond the moment it is inflicted.[38] Shay and Munroe listed seven common symptoms of their clients afflicted by moral injury: altered affect regulation; altered consciousness; altered self-perception—including a sense of helplessness, shame, guilt, and self-blame; altered perception; altered relations with others, such as repeatedly searching for a rescuer; altered systems of meaning; and somatization.[39]

Where previous terminology such as "soldier's heart" focused on somatic effects[40] and current terminology like PTSD focuses on the psycho-somatic symptoms and hyper-arousal of veterans,[41] moral injury focuses on the moral and social dimensions of the postwar experience. By describing the postwar experience of veterans in terms of moral injury, Shay and Munroe understood the loss of capacity for social trust as the key manifestation of the psychological injuries endured as a result of war.[42] As Shay said, "The essential injuries in combat PTSD are moral and social and so the central treatment must be moral and social. The best treatment restores control to the survivor and actively encourages communalization of the trauma. Healing is done *by* survivors, not *to* survivors."[43]

---

[36] Shay, "Moral Injury," 183.
[37] Shay and Munroe, "Group and Milieu Therapy for Veterans," 392.
[38] Shay, *Achilles in Vietnam*, 6.
[39] Shay and Munroe, "Group and Milieu Therapy for Veterans," 392–393.
[40] Kathleen Logothetis Thompson, "Healing the Unseen Wounds of War: Treating Mental Trauma in the Civil War and the Great War," in *Wars Civil and Great: The American Experience in the Civil War and World War I*, ed. David J. Silbey and Kanisorn Wongsrichanalai (Lawrence: University Press of Kansas, 2023), 176–177.
[41] Suzanne Gordon, *The Battle for Veterans' Healthcare: Dispatches from the Front Lines of Policy Making and Patient Care* (Ithaca: Cornell University Press, 2017), 75–78. American Psychiatric Association, *Diagnostic and Statistical Manual of Mental Disorders*, 5th edition, revised text (Arlington, VA: American Psychiatric Association, 2022), F43.10, doi.org/10.1176/appi.books.9780890425787.x07_Trauma_and_Stressor_Related_Disorders.
[42] Shay and Munroe, "Group and Milieu Therapy for Veterans," 392.
[43] Shay, *Achilles in Vietnam*, 179.

Following Shay's definition of moral injury, a variety of scholars and clinicians have continued to develop moral injury from a variety of contexts beyond the battlefield.[44] There are two common themes in new definitions I would like to emphasize as points of development. The first theme is typified by Christopher Hansen. Hansen described the experience of moral injury as having two parts: 1) the personal transgression of one's own moral values; 2) the betrayal, by "a person in leadership, of an ideal, or a cause."[45] Those who experience moral injury experience conflicts at both the personal and social levels of moral agency as well as a conflict between these two parts. Shay argued that these conflicts relate to the experiences of paranoia and difficulty relating to others with whom one previously had an intimate relationship those who experience moral injury tend to suffer.[46] Defining the postwar experience in this way creates an account that identifies not only conflict or distress at the level of personal moral agency but also at the social level as well as in the interplay between the personal and social dimensions of moral agency.

Second, contemporary definitions of moral injury have clarified the locus point of the injury. Through clinical practice and reflection, this locus point has come to be understood as the human person's self-identity. In "The Trauma of Moral Injury: Beyond the Battlefield," Eileen Dombo and others argue that when chosen and executed intentionally, behavior is understood to be an extension of the self. To choose an action one believes to be immoral can result in negative self-appraisals. Due to the intense and traumatic context of moral injuries, these negative self-appraisals threaten the integrity of the human person's moral schema and result in difficulty navigating the world. In Dombo, Gray, and Early's clinical experience and research, the injury does not terminate in the past. In fact, the injury is perpetuated through experiences of guilt and shame.[47] By identifying moral injuries as harming the human person's self-identity, Dombo, Early, and Gray account for both moral injury's threat to the integrity of the human person's moral schema and the experience of "damage to the cognitive structure of the moral self."[48]

---

[44] For more on other contexts for moral injury in addition to war, I recommend the following: Eileen A. Dombo, Cathleen Gray, and Barbara P. Early, "The Trauma of Moral Injury: Beyond the Battlefield," *Journal of Religion & Spirituality in Social Work: Social Thought* 32, no. 3 (2013): 202–206, doi.org/10.1080/15426432.2013.801732.
[45] Christopher Hansen, "Glimmers of the Infinite: The Tragedy of Moral Injury," *Theology and Science: A New Theological Anthropology for Developing Resiliency and Healing from Combat* 17, no. 1 (2019): 65, doi.org/10.1111/dial.12454.
[46] Shay, *Achilles in Vietnam*, 33–34.
[47] Dombo, Gray, and Early, "The Trauma of Moral Injury," 200–202.
[48] Dombo, Gray, and Early, "The Trauma of Moral Injury," 202.

MORAL INJURY AND CONSCIENCE

While the previous section presents various descriptions of moral injury based on first-person accounts, this section—following Coblentz—seeks to identify patterns among them. One way I see scholars accounting for the patterns in first-person accounts of moral injury is by relating the experience to conscience. While conscience is a concept more properly at home in theology, scholars from a variety of disciplines have taken to describing moral injury in terms of "conscience" to account for the depth and pervasiveness of suffering experienced in moral injury. Today's conscience-based descriptions vary greatly. While Marcus Mescher defined moral injury as an "abuse of conscience,"[49] Liana Lentz and others described it as compromising conscience.[50] By using the "Stress of Conscience Questionnaire (SCQ)," Erin Sugrue associated moral injury with a troubling of conscience.[51] Referencing Litz and Shay, K. C. Kalmbach and others described moral injury as a crisis of conscience.[52] Ben Onnik and others described moral injury as a "lasting insult to one's conscience,"[53] while Rita Brock called it the "trauma of moral conscience."[54]

Two recent articles developed the experience of moral injury in relation to conscience beyond passing definitions. The ability of their descriptions to account for fundamental portions of the narrative-

---

[49] Marcus Mescher, "Toward a Taxonomy of Moral Injury: Confronting the Harm Caused by Clergy Sexual Abuse," *Journal of the Society for Christian Ethics* 43, no. 1 (2023): 80.

[50] Liana M. Lentz, Lorraine Smith-MacDonald, David Malloy, R. Nicholas Carleton, and Suzette Brémault-Phillips, "Compromised Conscience: A Scoping Review of Moral Injury Among Firefighters, Paramedics, and Police Officers," *Frontiers in Psychology* 12 (2021): 639781, doi.org/10.3389/fpsyg.2021.639781.

[51] Erin Sugrue, "Moral Injury Among Professionals in K-12 Education," *American Educational Research Journal* 57, no. 1 (2020): 51–52, doi.org/10.3102/0002831219848690. For more on the Stress of Conscience Questionnaire (SCQ), see Ann-Louise Glasberg, Sture Eriksson, Vera Dahlqvist, Elisabeth Lindahl, Gunilla Strandberg, Anna Söderberg, Venke Sørlie, and Astrid Norberg, "Development and Initial Validation of the Stress of Conscience Questionnaire," *Nursing Ethics* 13 (2006): 633–648, doi.org/10.1177/0969733006069698.

[52] K. C. Kalmbach, Erin D. Basinger, Bryan Bayles, Randee Schmitt, Victoria Nunez, Bret A. Moore, and Richard G. Tedeschi, "Moral Injury in Post-9/11 Combat-Experienced Military Veterans: A Qualitative Thematic Analysis," *Psychological Services* 21, no. 2 (2023): 2, doi.org/10.1037/ser0000792; B. T. Litz, Nathan Stein, Eileen Delaney, Leslie Lebowitz, William P. Nash, Caroline Silva, and Shira Maguen, "Moral Injury and Moral Repair in War Veterans," *Clinical Psychology Review* 29, no. 8 (2009): 695–706, doi.org/10.1016/j.cpr.2009.07.003; Shay, "Moral injury," 182–191.

[53] Ben Onnink, Matthew C. Correll, Andrew Correll, and Terry Correll, "Psychotherapy's Role in Evaluating the Invisible Wounds of Moral Injury," *Innovations in Clinical Neuroscience* 21, nos. 1–3 (2024): 36–42.

[54] Brock, "Moral Conscience, Moral Injury, and Rituals for Recovery," 44.

phenomenological portrait of moral injury demonstrates the helpfulness of describing moral injury in relation to conscience. In "Toward a Taxonomy of Moral Injury," Mescher argued that considering conscience allows descriptions of moral injury to move beyond merely describing an entanglement of trauma to also give an account of estrangement from one's identity.[55] Second, in "Moral Conscience, Moral Injury, and Rituals for Recovery," Rita Brock gives an account of the experience of moral injury in terms of being unable to sustain clear distinctions between good and evil.[56] At the same time, these descriptions are at odds with each other. They reveal a looming issue for scholarship on moral injury. As Mescher argued, the relationship between conscience and moral injury has been "insufficiently considered."[57]

Rather than dismissing these accounts of moral injury because of their contradictions, I propose that when studied together they illuminate a thick description of moral injury's impact on conscience. This description proposes a pattern (as Coblentz describes it) conducive to theological reflection. Moral injury impacts conscience in four distinct moments. First, prior to moral injury the human person has made judgments about what is good and evil. She carries these judgments, made by conscience, into the experience of moral injury. These moral judgments are central to the experience the human person has of the world. While judgments are held in the deeply personal way described above, the human person forms and makes these judgments in the context of her engagement with a world that is social and in the context of her relationships with others.

From conscience, the human person then acts on these judgments in the context of her daily life and action. In the event of a moral injury, the human person faces a dilemma given her personal beliefs about good and evil. This judgment arises in the context of war and more immediately the command of an authority figure. The inability to maintain the relationship while choosing what one believes to be right poses an ethical dilemma: conscience is troubled. In moral injury when the choice is made to violate her sense of what is good, she transgresses her conscience. Given that her decision is heavily influenced by the particular context she faces, this transgression is a compromised one.

After the event that precipitates moral injury, the human person commonly identifies herself as "fractured."[58] As Brock describes, she

---

[55] Mescher, "Toward a Taxonomy of Moral Injury," 80–81.
[56] Brock, "Moral Conscience, Moral Injury, and Rituals for Recovery," 40.
[57] Mescher, "Toward a Taxonomy of Moral Injury," 91.
[58] Richardson, Lamson, and Hutto, "'My Whole Base and Moral Understanding Was Shattered,'" 463, 466–467.

is unable to sustain distinctions between good and evil. In the event of a moral injury the human person's conscience has been violated. This violation occurs in the context of a complicated relationship with others and their beliefs about what is good. After this event, she also has difficulty connecting with others. Put another way, her self-betrayal in the particular context of the moral injury engenders social mistrust. One of the tasks of recovery is then to foster a restoration of conscience. As the practices described above show, by regaining social trust and addressing the experience of self-betrayal, people who suffer moral injury may experience a restoration of their ability to sustain distinctions between good and evil.

By considering moral injury in four distinct moments—prior to the moral injury, in the choice that precipitates moral injury, in the effects of moral injury, and in recovery from moral injury—a coherent understanding of conscience emerges. Moral judgments and choices are made from the depth of one's being in a very personal way. In each of these instances, the choice that precipitates moral injury is experienced as implicating her whole self or self-identity. Additionally, in each of these stages the judgments about what is good or evil are made in the context of relationships with others. Judgments of conscience are made in a personal way in the context of social world and community. While wholly personal, conscience is not individualistic. Imitating Coblentz's framework, this understanding of conscience will guide the discussion of conscience in contemporary moral theology in the next section.

CONSCIENCE IN CONTEMPORARY CATHOLIC MORAL THEOLOGY

Today, conscience is employed in some of the most intractable disagreements in moral theology. As previously discussed, some of the most contentious debates in contemporary Catholic moral theology—like those about divorce and remarriage—have to do with rival definitions of conscience.[59] According to Cloutier and Koerpel, today's definition of conscience is a development of definitions proposed in the twentieth century.[60] In the latter half of the twentieth

---

[59] For more on the role of conscience in debates about *Amoris Laetitia*, see Conor Kelly, "The Role of the Moral Theologian in the Church: A Proposal in Light of *Amoris Laetitia*," *Theological Studies* 77, no. 4 (2016): 922–948, doi.org/10.1177/0040563916666824; Todd A. Salzman and Michael G. Lawler, "*Amoris Laetitia* and Catholic Morals," *The Furrow* 67, no. 12 (2016): 666–675.

[60] Cloutier and Koerpel traced the contemporary understanding of conscience and the law-conscience binary to medieval debates over Augustine's understanding of divine reason and will. They argued that understanding the law-conscience binary's genealogy is imperative to thinking beyond it. For the full genealogical description of

century, there was a turn in Catholic moral theology that aimed to create a "more personalistic, pastoral, and biblically based system of moral theology that [was] as concerned with one's fundamental relationship with Christ."[61] Essential to this turn was the definition of conscience in *Gaudium et Spes* as "the most secret core and sanctuary of a man," where "he is alone with God, Whose voice echoes in his depths."[62]

This definition of conscience proposed in *Gaudium et Spes* was deeply informed by the work of Bernard Häring. As Cloutier and Koerpel argued, in Häring's postwar European context recovering conscience was a necessary response to the two world wars and turbulent social changes of the 1960s.[63] Häring sought a Catholic moral theology that moved away from "'objectivist' and 'positivist' views of law to something more personal and pastoral."[64] In Cloutier and Koerpel's account, the personalist turn responds to the objectivism and legalism of the manualist tradition of the late nineteenth and early twentieth century.[65] The personalist turn was intended as a corrective to the way the late manualist tradition obscured the subject.

Today, contemporary Catholic moral theology owes much to this personalist turn. According to Cloutier and Koerpel, this turn is responsible for contemporary Catholic moral theology's account of subjectivity. For example, many key themes in Catholic moral theology, such as prioritizing the contexts of cultural traditions and socio-political factors of moral decision-making, are the result of this turn.[66] The contemporary emphasis on conscience is also part of this

---

the binary, see Cloutier and Koerpel, "Beyond the Law-Conscience Binary," 161–177.

[61] Cloutier and Koerpel, "Beyond the Law-Conscience Binary," 174; Robert J. Smith, "Conscience and Catholicism: The Nature and Function of Conscience," *in Contemporary Catholic Moral Theology* (Lanham, MD: University Press of America, 1998), 74.

[62] *Gaudium et Spes*, no. 16, www.vatican.va/archive/hist_councils/ii_vatican_council/documents/vat-ii_const_19651207_gaudium-et-spes_en.html.

[63] Cloutier and Koerpel, "Beyond the Law-Conscience Binary," 174. For an overview of Häring's theology, see Charles Curran, "Bernard Häring," in *Diverse Voices in Modern US Moral Theology* (Washington, DC: Georgetown University Press, 2018), 19–38. For more on *Gaudium et Spes*'s definition of conscience in the context of the Second Vatican Council, see the following: Charles Curran, "Strand Five: Second Vatican Council," in *The Development of Moral Theology* (Washington, DC: Georgetown University Press, 2013), 224–252; Massimo Faggioli, "The Battle over *Gaudium et Spes* Then and Now," in *A Council for the Global Church: Receiving Vatican II in History* (Minneapolis, MN: Fortress, 2015), 121–142.

[64] Cloutier and Koerpel, "Beyond the Law-Conscience Binary," 174. See also Smith, "Conscience and Catholicis," 74.

[65] Cloutier and Koerpel, "Beyond the Law-Conscience Binary," 169.

[66] Cloutier and Koerpel, "Beyond the Law-Conscience Binary," 175.

twentieth century inheritance. Cloutier and Koerpel understood the personalist turn's emphasis on conscience to be part of the post-conciliar movement away from pre-conciliar "juridical emphasis on ecclesial obedience to Church regulation."[67]

As much as has been gained through this personalist turn, Cloutier and Koerpel express reservations with how this personalist turn has been carried into the twenty-first century—especially regarding contemporary understandings of conscience. In the twenty-first century, contemporary personalist theologies understand conscience to be the source of moral agency.[68] Cloutier and Koerpel questioned these theories by quoting Alasdair MacIntyre:

> Within a personalist framework of conscience, how can one avoid the "self's self-serving presentation of itself to itself, a presentation designed to sustain an image of the self as well-ordered, free from fundamental conflict, troubled perhaps by occasional akratic difficulties, but for the most part entitled to approval both by itself and others"?[69]

Do contemporary personalist theories of conscience escape this concern of reducing conscience to "self-serving presentation"? This hesitation calls into question the authenticity of the authority granted to conscience. As long as conscience is defined in a binary against the objectivist law as the subjective authority of morality, it is not clear how this concern can be escaped. If this concern cannot be alleviated, the entirety of the personalist framework falls into question.

One way to address Cloutier and Koerpel's concern is to employ what Coblentz terms narrative-phenomenological portraits. In the narratives of moral injury presented above, I considered conscience in various moments of moral injury. When considered together, these moments resulted in an understanding of conscience simultaneously personal and social. This can be verified in the interconnectivity of the personal and social dimensions of human life experienced in various moments of a moral injury. In view of these portraits, conscience is neither atomistic nor individualistic.

The understanding of conscience that emerges from studying experiences of moral injury resonates quite well with the definition in *Gaudium et Spes*, no. 16: conscience is "the most secret core and sanctuary of a man," where one "is alone with God, Whose voice

---

[67] Cloutier and Koerpel, "Beyond the Law-Conscience Binary," 174.
[68] Cloutier and Koerpel, "Beyond the Law-Conscience Binary," 174–175.
[69] Cloutier and Koerpel, "Beyond the Law-Conscience Binary," 176. Alasdair MacIntyre, "What Has Christianity to Say to the Moral Philosopher?," in *The Doctrine of God and Theological Ethics*, ed. Alan J. Torrance and Michael Banner (New York: T & T Clark, 2006), 22.

echoes in his depths."[70] According to the Council, conscience is where the human person is alone with God and God summons the human person to do what is good and avoid evil. In this sense, conscience is very personal. At the same time, *Gaudium et Spes* does not neglect the social aspects of the human experience of conscience. According to *Gaudium et Spes,* conscience unites humanity in our common search for truth by making known the law God has written on human hearts.[71] Therefore, while conscience is where the human person is alone with God, it is also where she is joined to others. Like the portraits of moral injury, *Gaudium et Spes* paints a picture of conscience that involves an interplay between these personal and social aspects of moral decision-making and action.

When Cloutier and Koerpel raised a concern about the understanding of conscience's moral authority in the twenty-first century in terms of self-serving presentation, I understand them to be concerned about the lacking account of this interplay between the personal and social aspects of moral decision-making and action. When conscience is defined against law, it is difficult to maintain an account of conscience that does not isolate human persons and their moral judgments from each other. Put in the language of *Gaudium et Spes*, it is difficult for conscience as understood in the law-conscience binary to account for the way every human person is united in our common search for truth. Even though in today's law-conscience binary the personal and social dimensions of moral decision-making and action lack coherence and integration, this connection is present in the personalist proposal of *Gaudium et Spes.*

The personalist emphasis of *Gaudium et Spes* does not detract from the respective social elements of moral decision-making and judgments. The absence of the social dimensions of conscience in today's understanding of conscience "within the jurisdictional logic of the law-conscience binary" is a twenty-first century problem.[72] The personalist turn is not uniquely responsible for the law-conscience binary. Rather, by reflecting on firsthand accounts of moral injury and its resonances with *Gaudium et Spes*'s definition of conscience, twenty-first century Catholic moral theology can be understood to have not yet fully developed a theology that completes this personalist turn. Catholic moral theology today suffers from an underdevelopment of the social dimension of conscience—a dimension so instrumental to *Gaudium et Spes*'s understanding of conscience. To think beyond the law-conscience binary, Catholic moral theology in the twenty-first century would do well to develop an understanding of practical

---

[70] *Gaudium et Spes*, no. 16.
[71] *Gaudium et Spes*, no. 16.
[72] Cloutier and Koerpel, "Beyond the Law-Conscience Binary," 176.

reasoning and moral decision-making that accounts for this interplay of the personal and social aspects of conscience.

CONCLUSION

Coblentz's use of narrative and phenomenology in *Dust in the Blood* emerged from what she deemed as insufficient in theodical approaches' understanding of depressive suffering. In view of concerns and short-comings of today's definition of conscience, I have in view of Coblentz's success also employed narrative-phenomenological portraits to think beyond the law-conscience framework. Portraits of moral injury highlight the depth of interconnectivity between personal and social aspects of moral decision-making and judgments. This image is presupposed by the understanding of conscience proposed in *Gaudium et Spes*. While the law-conscience binary could be considered to be the result of the twentieth century's emphasis on conscience, I have proposed that the law-conscience binary is better understood as the result of an underdevelopment of this personalist turn and the respective definition of conscience proposed in *Gaudium et Spes*. By confronting the law-conscience binary with narrative and phenomenology, I have been able to propose a constructive way to make progress beyond intractable disagreements.

Catherine Yanko is visiting assistant professor at Belmont Abbey College. Her academic research focuses on post-conciliar Catholic moral theology. In particular, she has worked on fundamental moral theology, virtue theory, and the intersection of theology and psychology.

Christian Ethics, Trauma, and *Dust in the Blood*: Moving Toward Enfleshed Counter-Memory

Stephanie C. Edwards

Abstract: While presenting very real medical and religious challenges, theology tends to both over-psychologize and over-spiritualize mental health suffering. Inspired by Jessica Coblentz's theology of depression, articulated most thoroughly in her book *Dust in the Blood*, I expand her analysis to the field of trauma studies. Reading trauma with Coblentz clearly calls theology to account for its ongoing insufficient responses to real persons in pain. It also further exposes the metaphysical/ existential import of mental health writ large. To begin to address this void, I outline a Christian social ethic that calls the wider community to work for justice in contexts of suffering and facilitate spaces for potential healing when such justice is impossible. I call this ethic "enfleshed counter-memory." Christian theology, as read by Coblentz, requires an ethic that can respond within the "wilderness" as well as point beyond its borders. Such an ethic has the capacity to enliven theological scholarship and practice to rightly respond to the ongoing global mental health crisis.

D*UST IN THE BLOOD: A THEOLOGY OF LIFE WITH DEPRESSION* contends powerfully, and personally, with depression and its challenges to Christian theology.[1] Pushing "objective" boundaries, Jessica Coblentz blends her own experiences with classic theology, popular religion, and biblical wilderness narratives, resulting in a powerful assessment of depression theologically understood. As an ethicist, I take up the task of discipleship Coblentz lays out in her final chapter, not only how to read mental health distress as a theological wilderness experience, but asking: what do we *do* in the wilderness together?

To orient how I answer this question, I will follow Coblentz's model of authorial honesty. I have been a social worker for nearly fifteen years, working now in non-profit management in higher education. Most of my direct service experience is with adults in

---

[1] Jessica Coblentz, *Dust in the Blood: A Theology of Life with Depression* (Collegeville, MN: Liturgical Press Academic, 2022).

various marginalized positions, chiefly the unhoused, refugees and immigrants, woman-identified survivors of violence, and all the intersections therein. While I do not, and have never, held a clinical license, my scholarship is deeply interdisciplinary and embedded in practical training and experience. My theological writing focuses on trauma, exploring all that umbrella term holds: from chronic, medicalized Post-Traumatic Stress Disorder (PTSD),[2] to socially embedded and widespread suffering,[3] to the epigenetic inheritance of harm and resilience.[4] From this blend of research and practice, I am committed to process-oriented Christian ethics that centers the real people our theology claims to impact. While this article offers a loose framework for ethical action in response to mental health conditions, I encourage readers to question my proposal, stretch and bend it to meet their contexts, and set aside what is not helpful. As Coblentz puts it, "dissonances, too, can be revealing."[5]

This way of reading, writing, and acting stems from my work in mental health, where humility and flexibility are necessary attributes. Only through honesty and adaptability can we create contexts for healing complicated people, including ourselves. These values also cultivate environments of what bell hooks calls "constructive hope" in a deeply flawed world.[6] In theology such hope is founded in the long-term, committed struggle of the messy faithful to live into God's promise of liberation. It is this type of hope-driven community I find in Jess as a person and her research. In sharing her own story and analyzing it theologically, *Dust in the Blood* offers us all the gift of intersectional insight, destroying the false distance between who we are and what we write.

This insight is clearly stated in Coblentz's central claim of the sufferer's right to self-determination of meaning. Such agential empowerment is paired with the refusal to accept theological justifications of suffering via its eschatological resolution. As Coblentz outlines her task: "I seek means for theologizing meaningless suffering and for theologizing meaningful suffering

---

[2] Stephanie C. Edwards, "Pharmaceutical Memory Modification and Christianity's 'Dangerous' Memory," *Journal of the Society of Christian Ethics* 40, no. 1 (Spring/Summer 2020): 93–108.
[3] Stephanie C. Edwards, "Creating a Multidirectional Memory for Healing in the Former Yugoslavia," in *Healing and Peacebuilding after War: Transforming Trauma in Bosnia and Herzegovina*, ed. Marie Berry, Nancy Good, and Julianne Funk, Routledge Studies in Peace and Conflict Resolution (New York: Routledge, 2020), 89–105.
[4] Stephanie C. Edwards, "Imperialism of the Mind: Decolonial Theological Approaches to Traumatic Memory," *Political Theology* 24, no. 6 (2023): 544–569.
[5] Coblentz, *Dust in the Blood*, 126.
[6] bell hooks, *Teaching Community: A Pedagogy of Hope* (New York: Routledge, 2003).

without presuming that its meaning is necessary and inherent."[7] The dedication to process and precarity in meaning-making is the essential link between Coblentz's work and my own. It is the cornerstone upon which I build my proposed ethic and demonstrates how *Dust in the Blood* can shape a vigorous Christian ethic in response to mental health writ large. To this end, I first trace connections between Coblentz's work and trauma studies, showing how her insights on theology and depression hold wider implications for how Christian theology speaks (or does not speak) about mental health overall. Second, I introduce a Christian social ethic informed by Coblentz I term "enfleshed counter-memory." This ethic calls the wider community to co-create expansive literal and figurative spaces for healing—even if justice or resolution is impossible. Christian theology, as read by Coblentz, requires such an ethic that can respond within the wilderness of mental distress, as well as point beyond its borders. Third and finally, I briefly conclude with Black queer femme organizer adrienne maree brown's *Emergent Strategy*[8] to further enliven the path of action Coblentz calls for: a way to live in, through, and out of the wilderness, together.

COBLENTZ AND TRAUMA

Trauma is *not* depression, and to easily combine the two elides the particular nuances of the experiences. Collapsing distinct categories under the umbrella of "mental health" often leads to the ease of dominant theology's purported universal solutions to viscerally unique circumstances. This critique is well handled by Coblentz in part one of her book, so I will not spend time rehashing these intricacies here. I do, however, want to highlight that any false equivalencies between mental health challenges that may appear within this article are unintentional.[9] That said, there are resonances

---

[7] Coblentz, *Dust in the Blood*, 116. While the line between meaningful and meaningless suffering is blurry at best to all of us who experience pain, I agree with Coblentz that it is important, if not essential, to resist the imposition or presumption of extant meaning (*Dust in the Blood*, 106). An inherency bias that is the default position within theological reasoning around mental health suffering must be resisted to treat such experience in its fullness and respond to sufferers' testimony non-reductively.

[8] adrienne maree brown, *Emergent Strategy: Shaping Change, Changing Worlds* (Chico, CA: AK, 2017). Note: brown styles her name in all lower case and I follow her chosen grammar.

[9] Mental health and illness have a variety of definitions, but I generally use the World Health Organization as it is a leader in global service provision: mental health conditions/illnesses is a broad term "covering mental disorders, psychosocial disabilities, and (other) mental states associated with significant distress, impairment in functioning, or risk of self-harm," and mental health is "a state of well-being in which an individual realizes his or her own abilities, can cope with the normal stresses

between Coblentz's treatment of depression and trauma studies that reveal the need for a social ethic that reaches beyond one iteration of mental condition.

Individual Mental Health and Healing

"Trauma" has become a catchall term in popular discourse. Whereas depression holds a stigma that Coblentz identifies, often setting the sufferer outside of the "norm," trauma is frequently applied to everyone. While this may be easy to understand in our context of widespread turmoil and global pandemics, trauma's popular use and its diagnostic content differ greatly. At its most simple, trauma is any experience that overwhelms one's capacities.[10] Trauma is thus convenient shorthand for when one might feel like life has handed them "too much" or when one is struggling to understand a complex life experience. Though not diagnostically "trauma," this has become the cultural interpretation of its meaning. Medically, trauma is a defined experience that most people will have in their lifetime: approximately 70% of the world's population has been or will be exposed to a traumatic life event.[11] When this happens, our bodies create chemical responses to attempt to deal with the occurrence. These physical and psychological reactions to trauma are normal and part of the way our bodies have evolved to survive extreme circumstances.[12] When the responses do not pass, however, they become pathological and can develop into a myriad of post-traumatic disorders. Despite how many people experience trauma,

---

of life, can work productively, and is able to make a contribution to his or her community," World Health Organization, "The Global Health Observatory," September 2024, www.who.int/data/gho/data/themes/theme-details/GHO/mental-health.

[10] This is an intentionally over-broad definition, as US culture generally uses trauma language in this way. While there exists a multitude of ways to define trauma (such as by scale, type, symptom, or diagnosis), I utilize general language in this paper to avoid the reduction of trauma into only a medicalized definition (such as that from the American Psychological Association, referenced below). It should be noted that this is an imperfect choice, as trauma and all mental health disorders are very complex. However, I believe such a general definition has enough weight to hold a truth felt by many people, and thus motivating the social ethic that concludes this essay.

[11] Carolina Salgado, "Global Prevalence of Stress and Trauma and Related Disorders," *Global Collaboration on Traumatic Stress* (2024), www.global-psychotrauma.net/global-prevalence-of-trauma. Importantly, these can and do occur within the course of everyday life. Once considered fully "extraordinary," thinkers like Judith Herman helped reorient the understanding that "violence is violence and trauma is trauma" such that it permeates our cultural language.

[12] Responses include: gaps in memory of the event or an overwhelming inability to stop recalling every detail of the event long after its occurrence, increased heart rate/sweating, hypervigilance/anxiety, energetic or violent outbursts, and many more. These are often grouped under the "Post-Traumatic Stress Disorder" diagnosis in the US.

however, it is important to note that most people will *not* develop a chronic, disordered response.¹³

Trauma is thus distinct from depression, as it operates as an individual experience that *may* lead to disease, rather than fundamentally an experience *of* disease. That said, the sense of dislocation trauma engenders (whether one develops a disorder or not) is akin to that which Coblentz describes. This pervasive sense that one is separated from one's "home" (sense of self and meaning) unites diverse experiences of psychic interruption. This dislocation is most directly tied to a sufferer's experience of time. Where Coblentz beautifully draws forth the sense of *stasis* experienced in depression, trauma sufferers most frequently describe an intense *dynamism* in time—thrown back and forth between past and present, often unable to distinguish between the two.¹⁴ The importance of time is a fertile connection across psychological experiences, particularly in their ties to theology. Mental challenges in general ask theology to contend with time more expansively—to open up beyond the linear and into metaphors and practices that can hold the reality of time as experienced by those suffering.¹⁵

Such *ongoingness* in a person's life is one of the most powerful aspects of trauma that connects to Coblentz's descriptions of the nature of depression.¹⁶ Best practices from trauma healing methods suggest that long-term processes of integration are essential to foster healthy resilience.¹⁷ Resilience is a broad measurement of one's ability to undergo stress or harm and recover normal health. It is used as an indicator in post-trauma contexts to reflect on a person's capacities, as "healing" is variously defined and, for some, may never be "completed." Both trauma and depression ask us to reckon honestly with the ebb and flow of health and illness across our lifespans. We must recognize that an assumption of "normalcy" is just that: an often uninterrogated mindset that can, and will, be unceremoniously upended.

One practice that can create as well as demonstrate resilience is

---

[13] US Department of Veterans Affairs, "How Common is PTSD in Adults?," February 3, 2023, www.ptsd.va.gov/understand/common/common_adults.asp.
[14] Coblentz, *Dust in the Blood*, 45.
[15] Here, scholars such as Dirk Lange and David Turnbloom have played with the concept of liturgical time, John Swinton with God's time, and Madeline Jarrett with "crip time" to attempt to hold this truth within the Christian tradition.
[16] Coblentz, *Dust in the Blood,* 151 in describing Hagar, and *passim*.
[17] Juanita Meyer, "'Surviving My Story of Trauma': A Pastoral Theology of Resilience," in *Resilient Religion, Resilience, and Heartbreaking Adversity*, ed. Chris Hermans and Kobus Schoeman (Berlin: Lit, 2023), 153. See also Elaine Scarry, *The Body in Pain: The Making and Unmaking of the World* (Oxford: Oxford University Press, 1985).

testimony. Naming the suffering as felt by the person is shown to have lasting positive impacts. Rather than allowing systems, be they medical, juridical, or theological, to impose outside meaning on suffering, the sufferer should be encouraged to define their own story. As such, practices such as testimony and unrestrained lament are central to empowerment in mental health challenges. These methods help uncover ways persons can and have shown resilience *after* suffering as well as emphasize moments of resistance from *within* suffering.[18] Resistance is distinct from resilience, as resistance highlights one's capacity to act even in situations of extreme harm (what Coblentz terms "small agency").[19] Such resistance is routinely ignored in cases of both trauma and depression, as these instances are often morally complex and/or involve actions considered insignificant. Yet, naming both resistance and resilience is central to re-locating oneself during a period of mental disorder. On the individual level, Coblentz's work on depression demonstrates strong connections to trauma studies through its approach to time, dislocation, and healing practices.

Mental Health in Theological Context

Trauma is also distinct from depression in that it is fundamentally social. Trauma involves an "other"—be they particular or universal—bound up in the experience.[20] Depression as such often has no "perpetrator" and is defined within one's individual mind and body. I contend, however, that depression theologically understood is a shared condition. I align myself with the womanist scholars Coblentz engages, who highlight a relational theological anthropology. If God's image is present in all flesh, united in the mystical body of

---

[18] Jennifer Beste works on this with fundamental grace via Rahner with victim/survivors of sexual assault in *God and the Victim: Traumatic Intrusions on Grace and Freedom* (Oxford: Oxford University Press, 2007). These practices are theologically tied to Coblentz's discussion of "salvation, not liberation; incorporation, not cure" (*Dust in the Blood*, 186–189). The now-classic work on testimony and trauma narratives can be found in S. Felman and D. Laub, *Testimony: Crises of Witnessing in Literature, Psychoanalysis, and History* (New York: Routledge, 1992).

[19] Funlola Olojede, "Resilience and Resistance in the Book of Job: An African Socio-Economic Hermeneutical Reading," in *Resilient Religion, Resilience, and Heartbreaking Adversity*, 142. The author is presenting African Biblical Hermeneutics (ABH) as a distinctly decolonial act, socially engaged and attentive to moving the center of interpretation to a resistant and resilient Black theology. See also Coblentz, *Dust in the Blood*, 189.

[20] Trauma is not exclusively experienced in situations of interpersonal or social harm (e.g., war, sexual assault, violence), but also through accidents, natural disasters, or other situations for which there is no direct "offender" but rather a shared experience of suffering. All forms of trauma, therefore, while diverse are social.

Christ, then all iterations of individual embodiment maintain a social component.[21] Therefore, our treatment of mental health has theological as well as ethical ramifications. Not only do our attitudes and behaviors directly result in the availability or lack of healthcare resources and community support, they also shape how the sufferer views and relates themselves and their experience to God. In this way, both trauma and depression ask us to reckon with how we are bound up in the suffering of another and take seriously how such suffering can be alleviated as a matter of faith as well as justice.

This is not an easy task. Akin to how Coblentz describes the wilderness of depression, trauma reveals complexity rather than universalizes experience.[22] Critics of trauma discourse, however, rightly name the tendency to use it as a stand-in for all hardship.[23] This is particularly troubling for theologian Jennifer Beste, who calls out this universalizing behavior within the Catholic Church in response to the clergy sex abuse crisis.[24] She argues that, even though

> the narrative of a "traumatized church" can be compelling because the vivid language and images connected with trauma can resonate with many people's sense of horror at the reality of clergy sexual abuse . . . it also invites hope that, given our traumatic paralysis, God will respond to our prayers to heal and redeem the body of Christ so that the church can restore its good name, integrity, and positive influence in the world.[25]

Rather than activate moral agency in response to harm, she argues, the use of "we are all traumatized" rhetoric further disempowers victims and witnesses. It also eases our critical assessment of guilt and culpability for lay persons, parishes, and hierarchical structures, as well as perpetrators themselves. Further, it is problematic "that our hope for healing and justice in this scenario becomes more rooted in

---

[21] The work of M. S. Copeland, Delores Williams, and Eboni Marshall Turman explore this relational anthropology. This is a necessarily abbreviated summary, but essential to grounding the Christian social ethic I propose.

[22] Coblentz, *Dust in the Blood*, 133, "To correlate the biblical image of the wilderness, then, does not imply *one* set of theological conclusions."

[23] This ignores the diagnostic content, where we are now in the American Psychiatric Association's Diagnostic and Statistical Manual-V (DSM-V 2013, revised 2022), where the conceptualization of trauma and the diagnostic criteria of trauma were adjusted significantly; see Laura K. Jones and Jenny L. Cureton, "Trauma Redefined in the DSM-5: Rationale and Implications for Counseling Practice," *The Professional Counselor* 4, no. 3 (July 3, 2014): 257–271.

[24] Jennifer Beste, "Critical Reflections on the Discourse on a 'Traumatized Church,'" in *Theology in a Post-Traumatic Church*, ed. John N. Sheveland (Maryknoll, NY: Orbis Books, 2023), 39–63.

[25] Beste, "Critical Reflections," 49.

an image of a sovereign God who can choose (or not) to have mercy and infuse us with grace, and less rooted on activism and concrete actions."[26]

Such a misapplication of mental health labels within theology shifts us toward acceptance of our own apathy in the face of psychological challenges. We reach toward external grace in the name of traumatic impairment/paralysis, instead of enacting already graced actions toward healing and justice. Coblentz powerfully demonstrates how similarly misguided responses to depression create further harm and continue to alienate those in pain.[27] While there may be no direct "justice" claim in a case of depression, there remains a need for a theologically rooted social ethic that calls the community into responsibility to create the conditions for healing.

Social/Structural Components of Mental Health

In the mainstream US mental health sphere, the "curative" model rules.[28] This orientation emphasizes "curing" rather than "healing," giving primacy to hyper-individualized and medicalized solutions. While presenting very real medical challenges, *over*-psychologizing mental suffering ignores the metaphysical and existential import of the experience. Even though those aspects are frequently central to the sufferer, they pass uninterrogated.[29] While we must tread carefully here as theologians not medical doctors, as Coblentz rightly names, we cannot turn away from these larger contours of suffering. First, defaulting to the curative framework in theology functions practically to further burden the individual with sole responsibility for their own healing. Ignoring the existential aspects of suffering also hides or minimizes the fact that healing can and does occur in the face of an "incurable" bodily or psychological state. Finally, an over-emphasis on "cure" completely alleviates any responsibility for healing action from those outside of the individual experience. While this may emerge from a felt sense of valuing privacy ("it's your story"), a desire to get

---

[26] Beste, "Critical Reflections," 48.
[27] Coblentz, *Dust in the Blood*, chapter 3.
[28] From lay conversations to medical doctors to theologians, the medical model is presumed to be the universal arbiter of objective treatment, to the exclusion or diminishment of other expert fields. This assumption also ignores the flaws within medical care in the United States, and functions to hide the deeply imperfect ethical reasoning that determines a person's treatment under the curative model. These flaws include everything from implicit bias to resource rationing. See D. P. Gopal, U. Chetty, P. O'Donnell, C. Gajria, and J. Blackadder-Weinstein, "Implicit Bias in Healthcare: Clinical Practice, Research, and Decision Making," *Future Healthcare Journal* 8, no. 1 (2021): 40–48, doi.org/10.7861/fhj.2020-0233.
[29] Coblentz, *Dust in the Blood*, 23.

proper support ("you should see someone expert"), or the real knowledge of one's own limits ("I can't imagine"), our overall unwillingness to engage in the mental health of another often results in isolation, furthering what Coblentz terms the "unhomelike" experience.[30] While not the same in cause or presentation, trauma survivors experience similar cliché responses to those Coblentz identifies within depression treatment ("everything happens for a reason").[31] They also receive similar therapy, if they can access it at all, that assesses a broken "part" instead of healing an integrated, complex person. The US healthcare system is built to find solutions, and when one is not readily available or easily apparent, the person seeking help is often abandoned to their own devices.[32]

Beyond the systemic issues in healthcare provision, depression, trauma, and mental health are shaped by our cultural context. At first glance it is easy to assume we interpret health and illness from an objective assessment. Our evaluations, however, are deeply informed by what Emilie Townes calls "the cultural production of health."[33] This production hinges upon our understanding of morality—to oversimplify, health is a moral good and illness is a moral evil. These cultural and religious scripts are so deeply embedded that they often go unnoticed or are accepted as normal, right, and even just.[34] Such attitudes have real consequences, positioning the sufferer as deserving of their situation at worst or, at best, that the pain will have a purpose. This imposition of meaning is so ingrained that we perform it unconsciously, foreclosing any creative engagement that centers the sufferer's own interpretation. Following Townes's cultural construction of health, we must find new ways to interpret health, illness, and their theological ramifications.

In the social/structural realm, such interpretation is closely linked with practice. The methods of testimony and lament described above do not only serve an individual's healing. Such practices also move mental conditions beyond the internal world of a patient and into the

---

[30] This dislocation "breeds apathy" (Coblentz, *Dust in the Blood*, 84).
[31] Coblentz cites the major trauma and theology writers as pointing out this prevailing attitude (*Dust in the Blood*, 53).
[32] Alongside the prevalence of mental health conditions in the US (approximately 1 in 5 adults in 2021), there is a staggering crisis in mental health provision. In 2022, sixty percent of psychologists reported no availability for new clients, see Heather Stringer, "Mental Health Care Is in High Demand," *Monitor on Psychology* 55, no. 1 (January 1, 2024): 60.
[33] Emilie Townes, *Breaking the Fine Rain of Death: African American Health Issues and a Womanist Ethic of Care* (Eugene, OR: Wipf and Stock, 1998).
[34] Yochai Ataria goes so far as to argue that trauma is a "black hole" around which all Western culture orbits, and our continual exposure and lack of healing attention to trauma has damaged our communities (*The Structural Trauma of Western Culture* [Switzerland: Palgrave Macmillan, 2017]).

community as recipients or "hearers" of the story.³⁵ This is considered a practice of justice in response to mental distress by psychologist and trauma studies founder Judith Herman. Herman posits that moving toward justice is necessary, even calling it a "final stage of recovery."³⁶ In part, this commitment stems from Herman's reading of mental health through the lens of power. Understood through social power, personal suffering is never isolated. It is emboldened and enacted through structures that support harm and/or hinder healing. Herman argues that coalitional organizing and community building are the only proper response to hegemonic, violent power that positions some to suffer more than others. This relational response also calls entire communities to account for suffering and create specific, appropriate spaces for healing. While explicit justice efforts may be more or less appropriate depending on the context and content of mental health challenges, I maintain that Herman's proposal of community and connection is universally applicable. In Coblentz's metaphor, the emergence out of one's wilderness cannot occur without others.³⁷

COBLENTZ AND ENFLESHED COUNTER-MEMORY

Noting where Coblentz's work on depression intersects with trauma on the individual, theological, and social scale, I propose the ethical framework of "enfleshed counter-memory."³⁸ While this tool was initially developed in response to trauma, it holds potential for application across mental health challenges. Dedicated to relational, process-oriented methods, enfleshed counter-memory is meant to be used in diverse spaces. It seeks to cultivate action within liminal spaces, the "in-between" in which so many of us find ourselves. It is here where, as Coblentz names, we feel struck down "without any apparent reason [or] resolution."³⁹ Rather than waiting for the heavens to break open and offer perfect clarity, as Beste cautions, I

---

³⁵ Judith Herman, *Truth and Repair: How Trauma Survivors Envision Justice* (New York: Basic Books, 2023).
³⁶ Herman, *Truth and Repair*, 3. See also Coblentz, *Dust in the Blood*, 97.
³⁷ Coblentz, *Dust in the Blood,* 124. Coblentz also emphasizes that even in cases of depression, which are often chronic and have no exterior "cause" to remedy, we do not need to fall to tragedy and hopelessness but rather must turn toward community with others and God (*Dust in the Blood*, 163).
³⁸ A more robust exploration of this concept is found in Stephanie C. Edwards, *Enfleshed Counter-Memory: A Christian Social Ethic of Trauma* (Maryknoll, NY: Orbis Books, 2024).
³⁹ Coblentz, *Dust in the Blood*, 142. I also find Coblentz a stimulating dialogue partner in thinking through the lines between necessary situationist ethical reasoning, and universal norms for right action.

instead want to cultivate methods for building paths toward healing together. Here, Coblentz's work on depression is essential for testing the applicability of enfleshed counter-memory, and rigorously evaluating its utility for reframing how we assess, interpret, and heal mental distress.

Enfleshed counter-memory as a term is intentional and unapologetically theological: "enfleshed" in relation to complex and incarnational embodiment drawn from womanist thought; "counter" as the memory of suffering runs up against systems of power, drawn from Johann Baptist Metz; and "memory" as the essential category that unites considerations of mental health with Christian theology.[40] While seemingly just a turn of phrase, easily written off as a disembodied theological "solution," enfleshed counter-memory is meant to encourage concrete action. Through providing a broad tool for situational assessment, enfleshed counter-memory can begin to peel back the layers that surround mental health struggles and provide the theoretical basis to meet the challenge of suffering with committed hope and endurance.

First, enfleshed counter-memory centers real persons and our messy bodies. As Coblentz foregrounds her own experience with depression, so too must our ethical response. Centering the self-determining, honest expressions of suffering persons is the core of this ethic, and reflects best practices from the mental health professions. The orientation of "enfleshment" honors the bodily reality of mental health, placing our complex, literal flesh as a central connection to each other and God.[41] As it speaks with Coblentz's account of depression, enfleshed counter-memory draws forth an ethical orientation focused on engagement rather than completion, process rather than

---

[40] Memory is the faculty of human bodies that stores and recalls information. As such, it is where memories of suffering, and many mental illnesses, exist. Despite what our Cartesian inheritance may imply, a focus on memory does not ignore our bodies for the "true self" of spiritualized minds. Rather, I use memory as the psychologically agreed-upon site of action for healing mental distress. This is particularly relevant in trauma, as traumatic disorders interrupt and corrupt memory. Memory and memory studies constitute complex, interdisciplinary fields that cannot be treated here. I will note that as the site of recall of distress, and what Coblentz describes as a lack of capacity "to remember that life can be otherwise" from inside depression, memory is a robust site from which to construct ethical action. Further, memory is a theologically critical category, as in Jesus's Gospel injunction: "Do this in memory of me." There are exciting potential ties between enfleshed counter-memory and anamnesis, such as that explored in liturgical theology by Bruce Morrill, *Anamnesis as Dangerous Memory: Political and Liturgical Theology in Dialogue* (Collegeville, MN: Liturgical Press, 2000).

[41] I draw this term from M. Shawn Copeland, *Enfleshing Freedom: Body, Race, and Being* (Minneapolis, MN: Fortress, 2010). It is also informed by Mayra Rivera, *Poetics of the Flesh* (Durham, NC: Duke University Press, 2015).

success, and humility rather than triumphalism. These are lessons our bodies continue to teach us and all too tempting to ignore. Rather than offer a spiritual response to a visceral problem, focusing on enfleshment as our first ethical tool in addressing mental distress sets up a realistic framework for action.

Second, Coblentz beautifully and tragically points out that depression runs exactly counter to the cultural expectations of "success" and even "perfection"—particularly within theology. Through enfleshed counter-memory, we can see how such a counter-position is not to be feared. In fact, this position encourages us to recognize the lived reality of vulnerability in which we all share. Life is not a constant upward trajectory, yet this false vision is too often a pitfall within the Christian vision of resurrected life. Rather than ignore the wounds we accrue, enfleshed counter-memory encourages us to accompany each other's woundedness in a vision of Christ's resurrected body: a body that is both broken and risen.[42] The counter-position of memory of suffering emboldens this type of mystical-political discipleship. Here, we accompany each other in a vision of transformation not limited by earthly systems. In creating contexts for healing, we begin to make real God's promises of liberation.[43]

Finally, enfleshed counter-memory asks us all to remember suffering rightly, to remember such struggle *for life*. Christian frames of suffering are often rightfully questioned for ties to colonial modes of power, as well as overly spiritualized responses. The work of Spanish Jesuit and psychologist Ignacio Martín-Baró, however, offers an alternative for understanding enfleshed counter-memory in a Christian view of psychology. Liberation psychology, as defined by Martín-Baró, locates psychological experiences within their context, directly naming the sources of oppression and injustice that suffocate the possibility of genuine flourishing and often determine mental health or disease.[44] This orientation understands that mental illness "*is the product of both damaged neurons and the experiences of particular forms of relationship and community.*"[45] Memory in this

---

[42] My thinking here is influenced by Shelly Rambo, *Resurrecting Wounds: Living in the Afterlife of Trauma* (Waco, TX: Baylor University Press, 2017).

[43] Drawn from Johann B. Metz, *Faith in History and Society: Toward a Practical Fundamental Theology* (New York: Herder and Herder, 2007).

[44] Wayne Dykstra, "Liberation Psychology—A History for the Future," *The British Psychological Society*, November 14, 2014, www.bps.org.uk/psychologist/liberation-psychology-history-future. See also Martín-Baró's own account of the development of the field of which he is considered the founder in Ignacio Martín-Baró, *Writings for a Liberation Psychology*, ed. Adrianne Aron and Shawn Corne (Cambridge, MA: Harvard University Press, 1994).

[45] John Swinton, *Dementia: Living in the Memories of God* (Grand Rapids, MI: Eerdmans, 2012), 107, emphasis original. Memory, like mental illness, is not an empty concept. It

framework resists the hyper-individualized approach of psychology that often reduces whole persons to events or illnesses. Instead, it surges forward into praxis, "not an account of what *has been done*, but of what *needs to be done*."[46] Practices of memory are thus the process of contextualization of experience toward empowerment of self and community. This memory is active, resisting what many consider the "natural" way of things.[47] Positioned within a Christian worldview, Coblentz's work helps frame the pursuit of enfleshed counter-memory in recognition of God's transcendence and the call to "go and do likewise."[48]

DANCING IN THE WILDERNESS

Coblentz's theological treatment of depression offers a foundational conversation partner for, and nuanced challenge to, the applicability of enfleshed counter-memory outside of trauma. By no means do I claim that this initial sketch is the robust assessment necessary, but I hope it functions as inspiration for further engagement. As Toni Morrison puts it more poetically, I hope enfleshed counter-memory supports a theological model and method of a "dancing mind," here able to move in the wilderness.[49] Through exploring both depression and trauma, I maintain that a rigorous social ethic is needed in response to mental distress, to meet both the demands of justice as well as those of Christian discipleship. Enfleshed counter-memory is one such ethic, a framework that helps assess mental illness theologically as well as inspire practical action toward healing.[50] The goal of enfleshed counter-memory is by no means to

---

is constructed within contexts and with individuals that have specific purposes and ends for memory. This is why memory is praxis-oriented in my framework.

[46] Adrianne Aron and Shawn Corne, "Introduction," in *Writings for a Liberation Psychology*, 5–6, emphasis original. For a more recent account of this process in action, see Rosa Lia Chauca-Sabroso and Sandra Fuentes-Polar, "Development of a Historical Memory as a Psychosocial Recovery Process," in *Psychology of Liberation: Theory and Applications*, ed. Maritza Montero and Christopher C. Sonn (New York: Springer, 2009), 205–219.

[47] Coblentz, *Dust in the Blood*, 90—fighting "naturalization" of illness.

[48] Here Coblentz is playing with Hagar's story as a tragedy, one which pushes human understanding and which God transcends (*Dust in the Blood*, 167).

[49] This is also in keeping with the method of Karen Baker Fletcher, *Dancing with God: The Trinity from a Womanist Perspective* (St. Louis, MO: Chalice, 2006).

[50] To ignore the practical nature of enfleshed counter-memory is to misunderstand its purpose, and cooperates with the structural and personal sin that encourages trauma and mental distress. See Flora Keshgegian, *Redeeming Memories: A Theology of Healing and Transformation* (Nashville, TN: Abingdon, 2000), 152. The work for relational justice is essential to a Christian enfleshed counter-memory and inherently part of its definition. For consideration here, justice falls within three major realms (micro/individual, mezzo/community, macro/social) that map roughly onto the

impose meaning on suffering, as Coblentz rightfully cautions against, but instead to provide a framework for living in resistant and resilient communities. Such communities are the context in which future possibilities are cultivated—even the possibility of hope itself.[51] Hope in this sense is not a vision of perfect functioning or the obliteration of all earthly struggle. In enfleshed counter-memory, hope is created through shared vulnerability, compassionate care, and the pursuit of justice inspired by the Gospel.

Justice within enfleshed counter-memory is a life-long practice. It demands that we develop what activist adrienne maree brown calls *emergent strategies*. These are practical strategies that reach beyond any one experience of pain. They are aimed at building new worlds in recognition of our entanglement. As brown reflects on this shared task:

> The crisis is everywhere, massive massive massive.
> And we are small.
> But emergence notices the way small actions and connections create complex systems, patterns that become ecosystems and societies [and theologies]. Emergence is our inheritance as part of this universe; it is how we change. Emergent strategy is how we intentionally change in ways that grow our capacity to embody the just and liberated worlds we long for.[52]

In all her work, brown stresses the importance of *depth* over *breadth*. While social ethics are often aimed at social transformation, emergent strategies temper such an exclusive theoretical construction. Changing a social and theological imaginary is only accomplished through relational community work. As with the examples of testimony and lament, brown offers song and circle as necessary practices to reach the goal of transformation.[53] Through small-scale, long-term group work, our singing, sharing, and processing, we create the

---

multivalent usefulness of wilderness imagery Coblentz describes in chapter 5 (*Dust in the Blood*, 136–138). While these are by no means definitive of all possible routes, they are inspired by Herman's three broad phases of individual trauma healing: safety and stabilization, remembrance and mourning, and reconnection and integration (*Trauma and Recovery*).

[51] Coblentz, *Dust in the Blood*, 192, 194—inspired by her concept of "hoping that."
[52] brown, *Emergent Strategy*, 18, 3.
[53] brown, *Emergent Strategy*, 202, 257. Circle practices are commonly used in restorative/transformative justice as alternative methods of conflict resolution and accountability for harm. Only through creating alternative structures such as circles within our own communities, brown argues, can we even begin to transform our embedded attitudes and unjust power dynamics. This type of "movement healing" is also championed by modern Kingian Nonviolence, see Kazu Haga, *Healing Resistance: A Radically Different Response to Harm* (Berkeley, CA: Parallax, 2020).

contexts of trust that allow for surfacing, recognizing, and potentially healing mental distress.[54]

For Coblentz, such imagining does not ignore the "terror of the text"[55] (the very harrowing experience of complex mental health), but is rather an "expansion of possibilities for survival and improved quality of life."[56] Enfleshed counter-memory is, I hope, a part of this work: providing new ways to imagine our being that centers our contingent, entangled selves; encouraging practices of lived solidarity that challenge oppressive structures *and* provide soul-filling connection; and, ultimately, creating a way to intentionally hold suffering rightly in the Christian ethical life. To discover, as Jess puts it so well, that "it is a difficult place where God is."[57]

Stephanie C. Edwards, MSW, PhD, is executive director, Boston Theological Interreligious Consortium (BTI). She is a Catholic ethicist and a social worker, practicing diverse service delivery, grant writing, and nonprofit management for over a decade.

---

[54] Not all mental disorders can be addressed within these communal methods. While such methods can be used to structure testimony and lament for all, no matter their disability/experience, healing itself must be sought holistically, through networks of caring professionals, inclusive of medical doctors, social workers, psychologists, psychiatrists, and faith leaders.
[55] Coblentz, *Dust in the Blood*, 145.
[56] Coblentz, *Dust in the Blood*, 185.
[57] Coblentz, *Dust in the Blood*, 135.

How (Not) to Theologize Psychological Distress: Lessons from Thinking Across Conditions

Jessica Coblentz

Abstract: With appreciation for how Stephanie Edwards and Catherine Yanko apply insights from Coblentz's *Dust in the Blood: A Theology of Life with Depression* to theologies focused on other forms of psychological distress, Coblentz elucidates from their essays six insights or "lessons" to apply to the ongoing work of theologizing psychological distress. These lessons variously explore the relationship of different mental health conditions, mental health stigma, social dimensions of psychological distress, complexities of moral agency, epistemic injustice, and the place of Christ in the ongoing project of theologizing mental health.

LESSON 1: WE NEED TO SPEAK SPECIFICALLY, BUT NOT IN ISOLATION

WHEN I STARTED RESEARCHING THEOLOGIES OF DEPRESSION almost a decade ago, I was motivated by a curious lacuna in contemporary Christian theology. While there was much reflection on suffering and a small but growing discourse on trauma, I could hardly find a substantial treatment of depression. I knew depression was a reality far more common than what one might glean from academic theology, and so I began to wonder: Do we even need theological reflection on depression, in particular? Perhaps existing theologies of suffering, even these nascent theologies of trauma, suffice to address the theological issues presented by depressive experience. Would centering depression, specifically, shed any distinctive light on who God is and what God wills for our world?

I would not have written *Dust in the Blood* had I not perceived some need for a distinctively depressive account of our hope as Christians (1 Peter 3:15). This led me to pursue an articulation of Christianity that might be legible to those of us who inhabit, or have inhabited, the peculiar wilderness of depression. I strove to articulate Christianity in the native tongue of depression sufferers, one often seemingly untranslatable to non-natives and one sometimes rendered mute by the sheer force of this psychic pain. And I continue to champion theologies that center depression, specifically: I think we need more of them!

Thanks to some thoughtful interlocutors of the book since its publication, I have also come to see the hazards of developing a theology that emphasizes depression's distinctiveness. Andrew Prevot, for instance, has wondered whether stressing the otherness of the world of depression could mislead us into thinking that it is wholly unrelatable to those who do not experience the condition. What about the possibility of shared worlds, he poses, experiences that resonate across the struggles of depressed and non-depressed persons?[1] Distancing depression from other ways of being in the world could inadvertently compound the isolation already experienced by depression sufferers, he suggests. And it could justify what Edwards rightly names as theologians' common "unwillingness to engage in the mental health of another," which already contributes to the social and theological marginalization of depression sufferers.[2]

How to advance a theology of depression that honors the particularities of this condition without obscuring its resonance with other experiences or its theological relevance beyond depression has thus emerged as another important issue for my theological reflection. One valued gift that Edwards and Yanko offer with this roundtable is intellectual companionship in actualizing this kind of thinking across conditions. With their essays, they lead the way: by bringing *Dust in the Blood* into dialogue with research on trauma and moral injury, Edwards and Yanko surface possibilities for theological reflection across psychological experiences without collapsing the differences among them. They show how reflection on depression can reveal or inspire truths of broader theological relevance. In the process, they demonstrate how theological insights born of trauma and moral injury redound to other realities as well.

Their thoughtful essays prove an important lesson I carry forth in my scholarship on depression: though the range and particularities of mental health struggles necessitate that we speak specifically so as to avoid generalities about psychological distress and any one condition in particular, we need not do this in isolation. Indeed, there are broadly applicable lessons to be culled from theologies that focus on discrete

---

[1] Andrew Prevot, "Shared Worlds," in "Symposium on Jessica Coblentz's *Dust in the Blood: A Theology of Life with Depression*," *Syndicate* (August 17, 2023), www.syndicate.network/symposia/theology/dust-in-the-blood/.
[2] Stephanie C. Edwards, "Christian Ethics, Trauma, and *Dust in the Blood*: Moving Toward Enfleshed Counter-Memory," *Journal of Moral Theology* 14, no. 1 (2025): 82.

conditions, especially when we approach one another's work with the generous and collaborative spirit Edwards and Yanko exemplify.

I proceed by identifying several additional lessons Edwards and Yanko bring into focus or inspire with their essays, lessons that might guide the ongoing project of theologizing psychological distress. One might see these lessons as supplements to chapter 4 of *Dust in the Blood*, where I consider the moral and theological transgressions that result from imposing meaning onto another's depression and propose guidelines for theological reflection on this condition. That chapter bears the title, "How (Not) to Talk about Depression," and the title of this response is a nod to it.

LESSON 2: WE ARE RESPONSIBLE TO SPEAK, AND TO SPEAK RESPONSIBLY

Early in Edwards's consideration of how "insights about theology and depression hold wider implications for how Christian theology speaks (or does not speak) about mental health overall" is an incisive comparison of trauma and depression.[3] Her careful observations are vital for attending to all that is exceptional about the respective worlds of depression and trauma while recognizing what they also share—in her words, "time, dislocation, and healing practices."[4] With appreciation for the commonalities Edwards illuminates here, I found some of her points of contrast especially instructive for the ongoing project of theologizing psychological distress.

Edwards notes that "whereas depression holds a stigma . . . often setting the sufferer outside of the 'norm,' trauma is frequently applied to everyone."[5] Her subsequent discussion of trauma's relative ubiquity, both real and perceived, recalls recent news coverage of trigger-warning debates in our schools and viral trauma discourse on TikTok.[6] This coverage may seem a boon for sufferers and theologians of trauma, as anti-stigma campaigns often champion public awareness

---

[3] Edwards, "Christian Ethics, Trauma, and *Dust in the Blood*," 76.
[4] Edwards, "Christian Ethics, Trauma, and *Dust in the Blood*," 79.
[5] Edwards, "Christian Ethics, Trauma, and *Dust in the Blood*," 77.
[6] See, for example, Katherine Rosman, "Should College Come with Trigger Warnings? At Cornell, It's a 'Hard No,'" *New York Times* (April 12, 2023), www.nytimes.com/2023/04/12/nyregion/cornell-student-assembly-trigger-warnings.html; Olga Khazan, "The Real Problem with Trigger Warnings," *The Atlantic* (March 28, 2019), www.theatlantic.com/health/archive/2019/03/do-trigger-warnings-work/585871/; Jessica Bennett, "If Everything Is 'Trauma,' Is Anything?," *New York Times* (February 4, 2022), www.nytimes.com/2022/02/04/opinion/caleb-love-bombing-gaslighting-trauma.html; and Shannon Palus, "Why TikTok Is So Obsessed with Labeling Everything a Trauma Response," *Slate* (October 6, 2021), www.slate.com/technology/2021/10/tiktok-trauma-response-why.html.

and education as important priorities. Yet Edwards's observations about disjunctions between popular and medical understandings of trauma expose the potential pitfalls of the "normalization" or "universalization" of trauma—and other conditions.

Trauma's association with the kinds of emotional overwhelm experienced by the broadest swath of people sets up the public to overlook more severe, disabling, and persistent manifestations of trauma that affect a smaller number of us. And from this, ironically, more mental health stigma sometimes follows. The notion that, per Beste, "we are all traumatized" can function as an invalidating microaggression, one that minimizes the suffering of trauma survivors by suggesting that their suffering is really not so bad; to struggle to live with such trauma as well as everyone else allegedly does is therefore a personal failing, a sign of the survivor's immaturity or incompetence.[7] Meanwhile, reducing trauma to its most ordinary manifestations can obscure the public's perception of the *extra*ordinary work of healing some trauma requires, especially trauma at its most severe.[8]

Though trauma has exceptional standing in our public discourse, analogous normalizations play out in relation to other mental health conditions, making Edwards's cautionary analysis about the hazards of normalization relevant to theologians working on a range of psychological phenomena. I know firsthand that well-intentioned efforts to normalize depression can similarly play into stigma, for instance. A not-uncommon response to my own research is the assurance that "everyone gets depressed sometimes"—a line that always strikes me as a misunderstanding and belittling of the suffering I witness in depression research. The risks of normalizing mental health struggles take on even higher stakes when talking about suicidal ideation. Scholars of suicidality advocate for de-stigmatizing suicidality and suicide deaths *without* normalizing them, as normalization can deter experients and their companions from registering suicidality as an emergency and seeking out the life-saving mental-health interventions upon which people's lives depend.[9] As theologian

---

[7] For more on the role of invalidating microaggressions in mental health stigma, see Lauren Gonzales, Kristin C. Davidoff, Kevin L. Nadal, and Philip T. Yanos, "Microaggressions Experienced by Persons with Mental Illnesses: An Exploratory Study," *Psychiatric Rehabilitation Journal* 38, no. 3 (2015): 234–241, doi.org/10.1037/prj0000096.

[8] For a theological reflection on the demands of trauma healing, see Julia Feder, *Incarnating Grace: A Theology of Healing from Sexual Trauma* (New York: Fordham University Press, 2023).

[9] While not using the language of "normalization," suicidologist Thomas Joiner makes this point in another way in his advocacy for preserving fear of suicide: "For any stigma, the usual ingredients are fear and ignorance. If suicide is special in the degree to which it is stigmatized—and I and other believe it may be—then it is simply

Elizabeth Antus advises, we need to "de-stigmatize suicidal people without normalizing or romanticizing suicide."[10]

When it comes to mental health struggles, it is detrimental for depression and other conditions to be hidden away from the public eye and stigmatized as abnormal, but it is also not good that trauma or any other condition is so normalized as to be downplayed and misunderstood. Both shame-filled silence and careless conversation can do harm. This should humble theologians, especially those of us advocating for *more* theological reflection on psychological distress. While we have a responsibility to speak up about mental health challenges, we must speak responsibly when we do.

Edwards models for us how to speak to a broad range of experiences without flattening a condition, and for this, her direct acknowledgement of trauma's diversity and her descriptions of some of these variances are crucial. This requires us to speak from expertise and with specificity about each of the conditions we address—a task that builds on the first lesson of this essay. The cross-contextual exchange Edwards and Yanko model with this roundtable is yet another strategy for responsible theology, as it positions us to speak from our narrow expertise while leaning on and learning from one another's respective knowledge. Perhaps most obviously, we need to educate ourselves about the trappings of mental health stigma, which are more complex than what is typically conveyed in public discourse.[11]

LESSON 3: MENTAL HEALTH STRUGGLES ARE SOCIAL REALITIES IN NEED OF SOCIAL RESPONSES

Edwards offers another edifying contrast with her observation that "Trauma involves an 'other'—be they particular or universal—who is bound up in the experience. Depression as such often has no 'perpetrator' and is defined within one's individual mind and body."[12] I pick up and elaborate on these phenomenological and etiological

---

because the fear and ignorance are so great. Stigma about suicide should be reduced, of course, and it is a point of this book to do so, but I think it should be reduced via a decrease in ignorance, not in fear. I would prefer to leave the fear of death by suicide more or less intact. Fear can be quite healthy, and its absence can be deranged. Some of the most consistently fearless people are the most dangerous and disturbed" (Thomas Joiner, *Myths About Suicide* [Cambridge, MA: Harvard University Press, 2010], 4).

[10] Elizabeth Antus, "'The Silence of the Dead': Remembering Suicide Victims and Reimagining the Communion of Saints," *Theological Studies* 81, no. 2 (2020): 396.

[11] For more on this, I recommend Patrick W. Corrigan, *The Stigma Effect: Unintended Consequences of Mental Health Campaigns* (New York: Colombia University Press, 2018).

[12] Edwards, "Christian Ethics, Trauma, and *Dust in the Blood*," 79.

differences because they have far-reaching theological implications for these and other forms of psychological distress and can be misconstrued to distort our understandings of how depression and other conditions relate to the social worlds around them.

As Edwards notes, trauma has an identifiable originating cause or set of causes—what some call the "trauma event." This originating cause or set of causes continues to feature predominantly in the experience of trauma, as subsequent "triggers" or activators are often tied to the originating event. Following battlefield violence, for example, a traumatized veteran may be activated by loud noises reminiscent of weapons. The originating event is not just a past but also present component of ongoing trauma. Trauma's more-or-less discernable origin in something external to the person does not always spare sufferers of self-blame, to be sure, but it can make the interpersonal and structural realities of trauma more obvious. The trauma sufferer who survives sexual abuse by a Catholic priest needs personal psychological healing, but her situation also beckons responses that aim to restore her experience of interpersonal safety and structural interventions to prevent this kind of sexual and spiritual violence from happening again. In fact, these realms of healing often go hand in hand.[13] Thus while experiences of trauma are personal and subjective, the problem of trauma clearly originates from without; it is therefore more recognizable as a social problem in need of social address.

Because most depression does not have a clearly discernable, external cause or set of causes that continue to dominate one's experience of mental distress in obvious ways, the interpersonal and structural dimensions of depression remain much more elusive and therefore often go unnoticed.[14] Revisions to the American Psychiatric

---

[13] The scholarship of religious trauma brings into focus the entanglements of spiritual and other dimensions of trauma especially well. See, for example, Michelle Panchuk, "Distorting Concepts, Obscured Experiences: Hermeneutical Injustice in Religious Trauma and Spiritual Violence," *Hypatia* 35, no. 4 (2020): 607–625, doi.org/10.1017/hyp.2020.32 and Michelle Panchuk, "The Shattered Spiritual Self: A Philosophical Exploration of Religious Trauma," *Res Philosophica* 95, no. 3 (2018): 505–530, doi.org/10.11612/resphil.1684.

[14] One might assume that postpartum depression is an exception to this, as it is popularly presented as a direct byproduct of hormonal changes that accompany pregnancy and birth. Some research on postpartum depression complicates this etiological account, however, arguing that social constructions of motherhood contribute to this condition as much as, or even more than, biological causes. See, for example, Natasha S. Mauthner, "'Imprisoned in My Own Prison': A Relational Understanding of Sonya's Story of Postpartum Depression," and Paula Nicolson, "Postpartum Depression: Women's Accounts of Loss and Change," in *Situating Sadness: Women and Depression in Social Context*, ed. Janet M. Stoppard and Linda M. McMullen (New York: New York University Press, 2003), 88–112, 113–138.

Association's *Diagnostic and Statistical Manual of Mental Disorders*, the primary guide for diagnosing depression in the United States, have reenforced this by emphasizing that a presenting, external cause for one's depressive symptoms is diagnostically disqualifying: If the loss of a loved one results in what appears to be major depression, then it is, by definition, *not* depression.[15] This lends itself to individualistic characterizations of depression, especially under the influence of our Western biomedical milieu. Psychiatrist and theologian Warren Kinghorn observes how the biomedical model habituates clinicians and the wider public to conceive of depression as a problem *inside* the individual to be treated without concern for any external contextual factors.[16] Though this biomedical framework also prompts individualistic approaches to trauma, most clinicians carry out treatments aware that Post-Traumatic Stress Disorder (PTSD) has, by definition, external causes particular to the person's interpersonal and/or social context.[17]

In contrast to trauma—which, along with moral injury, is rather exceptional among mental health conditions for its definition *vis-à-vis* an external cause—depression is typically cast as a condition that originates and resides *within* the person, apart from anything in her wider social context. It is therefore much less evident that our understandings of and responses to depression should attend to social realities such as sexism, racism, poverty, transphobia, and homophobia. The same can be said for myriad other mental health conditions, from schizophrenia to anxiety to borderline personality disorder, also theorized as conditions that reside *within* the individual apart from her social world.

There is evidence, however, that social realities *do* contribute to, compound, and shape depressive experience and many of the other mental health conditions that tend to be thought of as maladies of the self-contained, individual "mind." My own interest in feminist psychology has introduced me to decades of empirical research connecting depression to poverty and patriarchy, for example.[18] But,

---

[15] See Coblentz, *Dust in the Blood*, 24–28.
[16] Warren Kinghorn, *Wayfaring: A Christian Response to Mental Health Care* (Grand Rapids, MI: Eerdmans, 2024), 83–86, 90–95.
[17] Kinghorn, *Wayfaring*, 48–49.
[18] See, for example, Dana Crowley Jack, *Silencing the Self: Women and Depression* (Cambridge, MA: Harvard University Press, 1993); Dana Crowley Jack and Alisha Ali, eds., *Silencing the Self Across Cultures: Depression and Gender in the Social World* (New York: Oxford University Press, 2010); Michelle N. Lafrance, *Women and Depression: Recovery and Resistance* (New York: Routledge, 2009); Janet M. Stoppard, *Understanding Depression: Feminist Social Constructionist Approaches* (New York: Routledge, 2000); Janet M. Stoppard and Linda M. McMullen, eds.,

as Kinghorn suggests, such theories and treatments have been overshadowed in the West by the modern, individualist biomedical milieu.[19] Reclaiming the social dimensions of depression and many other mental health conditions is thus a needed corrective.

To this end, I argue in *Dust in the Blood* that, especially among onlookers to depressive suffering, our willingness to suspend theodical questions about why God is causing or permitting depression can position us to investigate the interpersonal and social factors that cause or magnify the depressive suffering in our midst.[20] Letting go of theological justifications for the suffering of others can free us for another set of theological issues, such as matters of social sin. Edwards picks up on this with the proposed social ethic, which I welcome with enthusiasm.

Yet maintaining too stark an etiological contrast between trauma and conditions such as depression risks obscuring just how relevant Edwards's proposed social ethic can be for theologizing psychological distress beyond trauma alone. Though, unlike trauma and moral injury, depression is not diagnostically defined or phenomenologically centered on an external cause, there is growing awareness across depression studies of how interpersonal, cultural, and social-structural realities contribute to, magnify, and condition experiences of depression, as I noted above. In this research, depression is social as well as personal, albeit differently than trauma.

Edwards's exhortation to "enfleshed counter-memory" positions theologians to invest more attention in the oft-neglected social dimensions of depression and other conditions. It can, furthermore, renew appreciation for theologians who have already begun to break out of the prevailing individualistic frameworks to analyze mental health struggles as both social and personal realities. Edwards lifts up the contextual, embodied, and wholistic approach to health long modeled by womanist theological approaches; the centrality of Delores Williams in *Dust in the Blood* will make it no surprise that I see womanist scholarship as essential to the ongoing work of theologizing mental health.[21] Also reflecting the orientation of

---

Situating Sadness: Women and Depression in Social Context (New York: New York University Press, 2003).
[19] Kinghorn, *Wayfaring*, passim.
[20] Coblentz, *Dust in the Blood*, 203–217.
[21] Adding to the sources already cited by Edwards, see Christena Cleveland, *God Is a Black Woman* (San Francisco: Amistad, 2022); Monica Coleman, *Bipolar Faith: A Black Woman's Journey with Depression and Faith* (Minneapolis, MN: Fortress, 2016); Monica Coleman, *Not Alone: Reflections on Faith and Depression* (Culver City, CA: Inner Prizes, 2012); Phillis Isabella Sheppard, *Tilling Sacred Grounds: Interiority, Black Women, and Religious Experience* (Lanham, MD: Lexington, 2022); Phillis Isabella Sheppard, *Self, Culture, and Others in Womanist Practical*

"enfleshment" that "honors the bodily reality of mental health, placing our complex, literal flesh as a central connection to each other and to God," Tasia Scrutton critiques the biological reductionism too often facilitated by biomedical approaches to depression; analyzing the autobiographical comic strip of depression sufferer Marjane Satrapi, she demonstrates what we miss about depression when we fail to attend to the social and interpersonal realities of enfleshment in addition to the biological.[22] Exemplifying a willingness to embrace "counter"-cultural approaches to healing—to "accompany each other in a vision of transformation that is not limited by earthly systems"— John Swinton's study of voice hearing challenges readers to consider the positive theological significance of some voices and the potential losses accrued by experients when these voices are "cured" in accordance with prevailing conceptions of "mental health" in the West.[23] Elizabeth Antus's call to rightly remember the suicide dead for the sake of destigmatizing suicide and recognizing their inherent belovedness and dignity models ethical memorialization that "surges forward into praxis, 'not an account of what *has been done,* but of what *needs to be done.*'"[24] Edwards's social ethic gives us more reason to appreciate these and other socially attentive theologies of mental health and to bring them together in service of robust and accurate portraits of psychological distress and social responses to these conditions.

The juxtaposition of the essays from Edwards and Yanko is also instructive for considering how differences among psychological states may at times necessitate different social responses from theologians and our churches. As with Edwards's characterization of trauma, Yanko's portrait of moral injury shows it to be a personal experience with a social-political dimension. It is a "political wound" that results from situations of social constraint wherein a contradiction emerges between one's moral convictions, on the one hand, and one's chosen actions under the direction of an outside authority, on the other. This brings about kind of "moral fracturing"—a fracturing of one's moral self-identity. The sufferer is left struggling with guilt and shame about her own sense of moral complicity and a "loss of capacity for social trust." In another point of similarity with trauma, Yanko argues that recovery from moral injury—this political wound—must entail

---

Theology (New York: Palgrave Macmillan, 2011); and Chanequa Walker-Barnes, *Too Heavy a Yoke: Black Women and the Burden of Strength* (Eugene, OR: Cascade, 2014).
[22] Tasia Scrutton, *Christianity and Depression: Interpretation, Meaning, and the Shaping of Experience* (London: SCM, 2020), 89–113.
[23] John Swinton, *Finding Jesus in the Storm: The Spiritual Lives of Christians with Mental Health Challenges* (Grand Rapids, MI: Eerdmans, 2020), 119–161.
[24] Antus, "'The Silence of the Dead.'"

social remedies. And yet, whereas Edwards's paper emphasizes the work of justice as a necessary component of trauma recovery, treatment for moral injury often centers on group therapy.[25]

These divergent social responses to the respective social wounds of trauma and moral injury beckon reflection: To what extent do these social responses reflect differences in the social dimensions of these conditions? Might moral injury incite or even demand a social ethic of justice, too? Conversely, what is the relationship between the interpersonal healing that unfolds in group therapy and the justice work of enfleshed counter-memory in context of traumas? This last question is already alive in the wider field of trauma studies, as evinced by the latest book from renowned clinician and theorist Judith Herman.[26] As theologians continue to engage mental health challenges as social realities in need of social responses, we must continue to reflect on the kinds of social responses in order. While I exhort all theologians of mental health to take up this task, the concerns of moral theology and ethics may position scholars in these areas to lead this discernment.

LESSON 4: WE NEED TO CONTEND WITH THE SOCIAL, COGNITIVE, AND MORAL CONSTRAINTS THAT ACCOMPANY PSYCHOLOGICAL DISTRESS

Yanko's essay shows that mental health struggles are not the only human realities that have fallen prey to decontextualization in academic discourse. Her analysis of moral injury puts into relief the social dimensions of conscience, which have been lost in "self-serving" accounts of the conscience and their caricatures. Moral injury also exposes the dangers of legalism—a concern that contributed to the development of contemporary theologies of conscience, as Yanko recounts—for obedience to external authority is often a source of moral injury itself. These external realities result in the fragmentation of one's moral identity, "injuring" one's exercise of conscience.

While Yanko uses the experience of moral injury to intervene in debates about the law-conscience binary, it is notable that other mental health conditions entail analogous experiences of cognitive and social constraint that affect one's moral agency and discernment. Examples from other conditions evince the importance of Yanko's intervention

---

[25] Yanko's previous engagement with Jonathan Shay introduced me to this therapeutic difference. See Catherine Yanko, "Moral Injury and the Role of Community in Conscience Formation," paper presentation, College Theology Society annual convention, Denver, CO, June 1, 2024.
[26] Judith Herman, *Truth and Repair: How Trauma Survivors Envision Justice* (New York: Basic Books, 2023).

and the inadequacy of the anthropology underpinning these reductive views of conscience that "isolate human persons and their moral judgments from each other."[27]

Supporting Yanko's critique of overly individualistic portraits of conscience is Michael-Paul Cartledge II's discussion of the cognitive constraints that often accompany depression, for example. "Both cognitive psychological accounts of depression and first-hand narratives confirm that depression can often limit one's capacity to believe the clear presentation of 'truth,'" explains Cartledge.[28] "Realistic and rational thoughts become transient, and any attempt to modify the distorted beliefs, even with clear evidence, is met with resistance. At worst, depression leads a person to view herself as worthless and nothing more than a burden."[29] These observations lead Cartledge to interrogate right belief as the goal of Christian education, an aim that not only places depression sufferers at a troubling disadvantage but also advances what he deems to be a flawed view of sanctification that places undo onus on the individual for her transformation in Christ.[30] Applying insights from his analysis to the law-conscience binary bolsters Yanko's argument, for depression, like moral injury, can limit one's personal resources for exercising conscience: depression, like moral injury, can entail cognitive constraints that affect one's capacity for right belief, including those that contribute to moral discernment. Even if the constraints of depression are not so obviously "external" to the person, depression's cognitive constraints, like those of moral injury, are beyond the immediate control of the person.[31] Rather than blaming those experiencing cognitive constraint for their impaired consciences (Yanko) or heterodox beliefs (Cartledge), both scholars invite us to interrogate the anthropological assumptions that underpin our theologies and call for their revision.[32]

---

[27] Edwards, "Christian Ethics, Trauma, and *Dust in the Blood*," 72.
[28] Michael Paul Cartledge II, "Belief Through the Darkness: The Vicarious Humanity of Christ as a Theological Framework for Educational Ministry Amid Depression," *Journal of Disability & Religion* 28, no. 2 (2022): 101, doi.org/10.1080/23312521.2022.2097152.
[29] Cartledge, "Belief Through the Darkness," 100.
[30] Cartledge, "Belief Through the Darkness," 101–107.
[31] While acknowledging the distinctions between depression and moral injury, I also reiterate that social and cultural constructions inform our perception that depression is "inside" a person, whereas trauma and moral injury are conditions that originate "outside" a person. Insofar as we are relational creatures with inseparable biological, relational, social, and spiritual dimensions, what is "within" and "outside" us can be distinguished but not separated. See Kinghorn, *Wayfaring*, passim.
[32] For more on the cognitive constraints of depression, including a discussion of the importance of recognizing the agency that often emerges as a crucial dimension of

Meanwhile, aligning with the other pole of the law-conscience binary will not resolve the complexities that mental health challenges pose to our moral theologies. Research on suicidal ideation supports Yanko's resistance to this binary by troubling a singular reliance on the law as an alternative guide for moral discernment, especially in situations where conscience is hindered by cognitive constraint. Listening to the experiences of nine LGBTQ+ Christians who survived suicide attempts, Cody Sanders observes how church doctrines and more subtle, informal theological messaging contributed to their experiences of suicidality. As in instances of moral injury, Sanders's analysis shows how external authority—here, church "law" regarding gender and sexuality—can contribute to suicidal ideation and the cognitive constraints that constitute it—constraints that can impinge upon the suicidal person's moral discernment.[33] Put simply, the law can contribute to the cognitive constraints that hinder conscience. We can see, therefore, how fraught it can be to respond to the cognitive constraints of suicidality by encouraging the suicidal person to rely on church teachings to guide their moral discernment.[34]

Admittedly, our attention to experiences of moral constraint amid these conditions and their consequent effects on moral discernment and agency could backfire: The moral impairments of moral injury, depression, and suicidal ideation could be coopted as more reason to question the morality of people with these conditions, especially in a context of mental health stigma. Already, terms like "crazy" and "insane" are often used synonymously with charges of "immorality," as is evident in some public responses to the racist, misogynistic, and xenophobic rhetoric of Donald Trump's US presidential campaigns.[35] Framing moral injury as a "wound" to conscience or emphasizing the impairments to moral agency that accompany depression and suicidality could feed into the stigmatizing trope that mentally ill

---

survival (what I term "small agency"), see Coblentz, *Dust in the Blood*, 38–48, 189–192.

[33] Cody J. Sanders, *Christianity, LGBTQ Suicide, and the Souls of Queer Folk* (Lanham, MD: Lexington, 2020). For more on the "cognitive constriction" that characterizes suicidality, see Antus, "'The Silence of the Dead,'" 402–403; Joiner, *Myths About Suicide*, 45–47; and Edwin S. Schneidman, *The Suicidal Mind*, revised edition (New York: Oxford University Press, 1998), 51–66, 133–134.

[34] To be clear, neither Sanders nor I are suggesting that church teaching is an absolutely unhelpful moral reference for people in general or suicidal people in particular. The point is that some appeals to the "law" as moral guide overlook the damage that also sometimes results from some church teaching or its application.

[35] Patrick Kennedy, "Stop Calling Trump 'Crazy.' It Demeans People with Mental Illness," *Washington Post* (August 8, 2016), www.washingtonpost.com/posteverything/wp/2016/08/08/stop-calling-trump-crazy/; David M. Perry, "Stop Calling Trump Crazy," *CNN* (August 4, 2016), www.cnn.com/2016/08/04/opinions/stop-calling-trump-crazy-perry/index.html.

people are morally incompetent and thus *immoral* people—people incapable of responsible moral discernment and decision making. This, of course, need not be the case. But its possibility poses a challenge to theologians: how do we speak honestly about the complex constraints at play in moral injury and other mental health conditions while resisting this stigma?

Emphasizing a distinction between diminished moral agency, on the one hand, and immoral agency, on the other, could assist in this task. Such a distinction rejects the Western norm of the ever-agentive, autonomous self—the very same anthropology that bolsters individualistic views of mental illness as well as the self-contained conscience. Yanko calls to acknowledge constraints beyond the control of the individual herself—whether the "external" social constraints that produce moral injury and contribute to suicidality, or the cognitive constraints of depression (which are not disconnected from the social as well!). By moving us beyond this idol of the self for the sake of conscience, she also provides valuable tools for avoiding this trap of mental health stigma. Thus, to the benefit of all, we will heed her call to hold our moral theological reflection accountable to those who attest to the moral constraint that results from various kinds of cognitive and social factors.

LESSON 5: LISTENING TO EXPERIENCES OF PSYCHOLOGICAL DISTRESS REQUIRES RECKONING WITH EPISTEMIC INJUSTICE

Adding to the appeal of first-person narratives and phenomenology that informed my previous research on depression, Yanko's essay convinces me that the ongoing work of theologizing psychological distress must include first-person narrative and phenomenology in addition to—if not more than—the "thin" descriptions that dominate the psychological sciences and psychiatric medicine. Her thick description of moral injury concretely demonstrates the inadequacies of theologies built on thin accounts of human experience.[36] In doing so, she shows that thin descriptions leave us ill equipped not only to address psychological struggles such as moral injury but also to generate relevant theologies that pertain to a much wider range of human realities, including conscience.

Importantly, too, theology's incorporation of first-person narratives, or testimonies, has potential not only to enrich our

---

[36] Yanko, with other scholars, uses the language of "thick" description to refer to first-person narratives and phenomenologies of human experience. This is often contrasted with "thin" descriptions that, in the words of John Swinton, provide "the minimum amount of information necessary to describe a situation and context" (Swinton, *Finding Jesus in the Storm*, 14).

scholarship but also to support the experients who offer them. As Edwards notes regarding contexts of trauma, "One practice that can create as well as demonstrate resilience is testimony. Naming the suffering as it is felt by the person is shown to have lasting positive impacts. Rather than allowing systems, be they medical, juridical, or theological, to impose outside meaning on suffering, the sufferer should be encouraged to define their own story."[37]

Some challenges will accompany greater engagement with first-person narrative and phenomenologies in our theological work, however. John Swinton identifies one such challenge in his turn to phenomenology, noting that a great deal of listening time is required for generating thick descriptions of mental health. This is the case whether one is collecting first-person narratives by listening to experients in real time or gathering disparate narratives and phenomenologies from previously published sources. For a description of moral injury, trauma, or depression, relying on a dictionary definition or diagnostic manual is far more efficient.

Yet even with the will and the time, theologians face another challenge in actualizing Yanko's call to engage first-person narratives and phenomenologies, this one concerning the prejudices and conceptual resources that result in what philosophers call epistemic injustice. Philosopher Miranda Fricker first theorized epistemic injustice as a form of social injustice in which someone is harmed in their capacity as a knower.[38] Her original analysis focused on two central features of this injustice. First, testimonial injustice arises when "prejudice causes a hearer to deflate the credibility of a speaker's word."[39] This deflation of creditability results from social bias. A woman visibly upset as she recounts a transgression against her may be discredited by listeners who, consciously or unconsciously, filter her testimony through the stereotype that women are overly emotional and therefore less reasonable and reliable narrators. She may be unjustly discredited by her hearers as a result.

Often serving as an underlying context for testimonial injustice, hermeneutical injustice is the second dimension of epistemic injustice. Hermeneutical injustice occurs when "a gap in collective interpretative resources puts someone at an unfair disadvantage when it comes to making sense of their social experiences."[40] Fricker famously uses the history of sexual harassment to illustrate this phenomenon.[41] The

---

[37] Edwards, "Christian Ethics, Trauma, and *Dust in the Blood*," 79.
[38] Miranda Fricker, *Epistemic Injustice: Power and the Ethics of Knowing* (New York: Oxford University Press, 2007), 20.
[39] Fricker, *Epistemic Injustice*, 1.
[40] Fricker, *Epistemic Injustice*, 1.
[41] Fricker, *Epistemic Injustice*, 149–152.

experience of what we today call "sexual harassment" occurred and often troubled victims, some of whom attempted to communicate about it long before the term "sexual harassment" was developed, widely known, or codified into US law. Yet because there was no collective concept of "sexual harassment"—due in part to the systemic marginalization of women in public life—these victims unjustly lacked the hermeneutical resources necessary to understand and effectively communicate about the experience. Returning to the aforementioned example, the woman visibly upset as she recounts a transgression against her may be unjustly harmed as a knower because of social stereotypes that call into question her knowledge and judgement (testimonial injustice) *and* also because she is speaking about a kind of transgression—say, sexual harassment—in a context where there was no such language or concept shared among herself and those to whom she is speaking (hermeneutical injustice).

These and other features of epistemic injustice reveal the social politics of knowing—of speaking and being understood. Dedicating our good will and time to hearing first-person narratives and phenomenological accounts of experience will not ensure that we escape testimonial and hermeneutical injustices, for these realities result primarily from collective ideologies and structures that shape our personal encounters with others' experiences, interpretations, and truth claims. While a wide range of social prejudices engender testimonial injustice and an array of experiences lack adequate recognition and theorization, resulting in hermeneutical injustice, this roundtable's focus on psychological distress compels me to emphasize the need to attend to the epistemic injustice often experienced by those with mental health challenges: if we are going to properly revere their credibility as knowers, then we need to heed and resist the epistemic injustice so often encountered by those of us who live with mental illness.[42]

Karen Newbigging and Julie Ridley warn that "people experiencing mental distress are particularly vulnerable to epistemic injustices as a consequence of deeply embedded social stigma resulting in *a priori* assumptions of irrationality and unreliability such

---

[42] Note that because people do not exist in a vacuum, the epistemic injustice faced by those experiencing psychological distress often intersects with other forms of epistemic injustice. For example, I discuss how gender, race, class, and mental-health biases coalesced to engender the epistemic injustice faced by Naomi Gaines in "'She Keeps Shouting After Us' (Mt. 15:23): Contextualizing Mental Illness, Restoring Epistemic Credibility, Expanding Care," in *Oxford Handbook on Theological Bioethics*, ed. Warren Kinghorn, John Berkman, and Robyn Elizabeth Boeré (New York: Oxford University Press), forthcoming.

that their knowledge is often discounted and downgraded."[43] Meanwhile, modern mental healthcare contexts often invest healthcare providers with epistemic privilege that disadvantages patients as knowers. "This privilege is accorded by virtue of their training, expertise, or third-person psychology, such that they occupy the epistemically privileged role of assessing which testimonies and interpretations to act upon, as well as deciding what sorts of testimonies to receive, from whom, what form they can take, and so on," explain philosophers Havi Carel and Ian James Kidd.[44] As such, when a person's first-person narration and interpretation of depression or trauma conflicts with the psychological establishment, social prejudice already disposes hearers to discredit the mentally ill person in favor of her clinician's take. This bias will incline our hearing regardless of the content of the sufferer's testimony.

Bringing first-person narratives and phenomenologies of psychological distress into our theologies will help to affirm the epistemic credibility of those with these conditions. It may also help the church develop hermeneutical resources for talking about psychological distress that our communities currently lack to the unjust disadvantage of experients. This is, in essence, what I attempted to do by centering first-person narratives and phenomenologies of depression in *Dust in the Blood*. Still relatively unfamiliar with the scholarship of epistemic injustice at the time, however, I did not theorize this methodological move with the tools of this philosophical discourse.[45] I am convinced that those of us who strive to center the voices of experients in our theologies henceforth will be better for thinking more with epistemic justice and the socio-political valence it brings to this methodological move, as some theologians of mental health have already begun to demonstrate.[46] We need, for instance, to anticipate and resist the social prejudices that we, as socially imbedded

---

[43] Karen Newbigging and Julie Ridley, "Epistemic Struggles: The Role of Advocacy in Promoting Epistemic Justice and Rights in Mental Health," *Social Science and Medicine* 219 (2018): 36.

[44] Havi Carel and Ian James Kidd, "Epistemic Injustice in Healthcare: A Philosophical Analysis," *Medicine, Health Care, and Philosophy* 17, no. 4 (April 17, 2014): 534–535.

[45] I am indebted to Erin Kidd, whose work on feminist theology and epistemic injustice inspired my interest in this area of feminist philosophy and demonstrates its importance for and beyond theologies of psychological distress. See Erin Kidd, "A Feminist Theology of Testimony," *Theological Studies* 83, no. 3 (2022): 424–442, doi.org/10.1177/00405639221117237.

[46] See Christopher Cook, *Hearing Spiritual Voices: Medieval Mystics, Meaning, and Psychiatry* (London: T&T Clark, 2023), 101–110; Swinton, *Finding Jesus in the Storm*, 145–147, 176, 180–181; Anastasia Philippa Scrutton, "Epistemic Injustice and Mental Illness," *The Routledge Handbook of Epistemic Injustice*, ed. Ian James Kidd, José Medina, Gaile Pohlhaus, Jr. (New York: Routledge, 2017), 347–355.

theologians, are already disposed to bring to the testimonies of the mentally ill. Those of us who live with these conditions are not exempt from these biases. Yanko's essay suggests that if we ignore the rich portraits of human experience advanced in first-person narratives in phenomenology—or, as I note here, if we incorporate these accounts of experience without adequately contending with epistemic injustice—our theologies will suffer for lack of the knowledge brought forth by those living with psychological distress.

LESSON 6: WE SHOULD CONSIDER THE PLACE OF CHRIST IN THEOLOGIZING PSYCHOLOGICAL DISTRESS

I opened this essay by recounting my motivating conviction about the need for theologies of depression such as the one I advance in *Dust in the Blood*. I conclude this essay by raising a related question, one apropos of this roundtable and one that continues to preoccupy and inspire my theological work: What can Christian theology bring to our understandings of and responses to psychological distress? Behind this question is the recognition that, with the expansion of mental health discourse, awareness, and resources in recent years, those in the church, academy, and wider world can turn to any number of sources *other than* Christian theology to address this dimension of human experience. Perhaps identifying the distinct potential of Christian theology will help theologians focus our efforts and articulate to various publics theology's potential for enriching our lives together. On the one hand, the aforementioned lessons from Edwards and Yanko already prove the generativity of theologies of psychological distress; there is much on offer in these two essays alone. On the other hand, there is much more theological work on psychological distress that remains to be done, as I have also tried to demonstrate here. Pondering what Christian theology, in particular, can bring to the diversity of mental health struggles in our midst may help us move forward intentionally and effectively.

The revelation of Jesus Christ is one place to begin an articulation of Christian theology's potential for a distinct contribution. Yet I am struck by the fact that in the essays from Yanko and Edwards as well as in my own book, *Dust in the Blood*, there is relatively little explicit engagement with the person of Christ. This presents an opportunity to build on and expand our theologies of psychological distress further. Hence, in the remainder of my response, I consider how Christ can enrich our shared theological endeavor.

Mindful that the absence of explicit discussions of Christ need not mean that Christ is wholly absent from this roundtable and other theological texts that focus on different figures and sources, we can already recognize in the essays from Edwards and Yanko an incarnational sensibility that informs their affirmation of the body as sacred and that recognizes its struggles against sin and suffering to be of upmost concern to God and God's followers. On this, M. Shawn Copeland's contemporary classic *Enfleshing Freedom* reminds us that the life, death, and resurrection of Christ reveals that bodies matter—especially suffering, marginalized bodies. She shows that taking suffering bodies seriously—in their pain and their freedom—necessarily follows from the revelation of Christ, who enfleshed God's love and concern for bodies in his word and action and in so doing modeled it for all who follow him.[47] Copeland's work provides a Christological buttress for the centrality of the body in the ethic of "enfleshed counter-memory" that Edwards extends to theologies of psychological distress and for the methodological centrality of embodied experience that Yanko elucidates from *Dust in the Blood* and applies to debates about the law-conscience binary.

Considering the revelation of Jesus in the Scriptures is another means by which we can further elucidate the significance of Christ for mental health challenges. Several readers of *Dust in the Blood* have invited me to reflect more on how Jesus's wilderness experiences might enrich the interpretation of depression as a wilderness experience that I advance in the book, and so I pass on this invitation to Edwards, Yanko, and our roundtable readers: How might the Jesus of Scripture enrich our theological reflections on psychological distress?

For instance, Yanko's essay proposes a view of conscience that is neither hyper-individualistic nor uncritically submissive to the law. Jesus of Nazareth was a figure who both revered the law and at times challenged it—in obedience to his own conscience, we might assume. In view of how experiences of moral injury expose the limits of our more reductive treatments of conscience, might some of the biblical stories of Jesus—his picking of grain on the Sabbath (Mark 2:23–28, Matthew 12:1–8, Luke 6:1–5) or healing of the man with the withered hand (Mark 3:1–6, Matthew 12:9–14, Luke 6:6–11), for example—help us develop Yanko's corrective, constructive vision of conscience?[48]

Could stories of Jesus likewise enrich the sketch of "enfleshed counter-memory" advanced by Edwards? No scene seems a more fitting place to start than the Last Supper (Mark 14:12–25, Matthew 26:17–30, Luke 22:7–38), when Jesus and his disciples memorialized the Passover, a memory of past suffering and salvation that beckons God's continued call to participate in a praxis of liberation over and against worldly expectations and the status quo. "Like millions of

---

[47] M. Shawn Copeland, *Enfleshing Freedom: Body, Race, and Being* (Minneapolis, MN: Fortress, 2010).
[48] Thanks to Paul Schutz for suggesting these examples.

Jews before him and millions of Jews after him, in this ritual meal Jesus acknowledged, blessed, and praised God who, through mighty acts, chose, liberated, guided, protected, nourished, sustained, and ennobled a people," recounts Copeland.[49] Because this practice of counter-memory in Jesus's life emboldened him to continue to work for justice in the hours that followed, even to death, this Gospel scene should spur Christians to consider how our own commemorative enactment of this meal in the Eucharist—another ritual of "enfleshed counter-memory"?—likewise spurs us to justice, what Copeland terms "eucharistic solidarity."[50] Might reflection on Jesus's Last Supper and our ongoing practice of Eucharist enrich the understandings of enfleshed counter memory we bring to bear on theologies of psychological distress?

As we continue the work of theologizing psychological distress and articulating what theological reflection, in particular, can bring to understandings of and responses to the psychological distress in our lives and communities, I am grateful to be in this work together. That there are ideas from *Dust in the Blood* that ring true for the work of Yanko and Edwards and the communities of mental health sufferers with whom they think means that we sufferers and theologians of depression are not alone in pursuing God and struggling for the right words to communicate about the God who meets us in our experience—or does not. With gratitude for and inspiration from Yanko and Edwards, I conclude with hope for the theologies of psychological distress yet to come. Let us continue to do this work together. M

Jessica Coblentz, PhD, is associate professor in the Department of Religious Studies and Theology and affiliate faculty in the Department of Gender and Women's Studies at Saint Mary's College in Notre Dame, Indiana. She is the author of *Dust in the Blood: A Theology of Life with Depression* (Liturgical Academic, 2022), and the co-editor of two volumes, *The Human in a Dehumanizing World: Reexamining Theological Anthropology and Its Implications* (Orbis, 2022) and *Women Responding to the Spirit: Selections from the Madeleva Lectures* (Paulist, 2025).

---

[49] Copeland, *Enfleshing Freedom*, 108.
[50] Copeland, *Enfleshing Freedom*, 124–128.

Book Reviews

Catholic Social Learning: Educating the Faith That Does Justice. Expanded Edition. By Roger Bergman. Eugene, OR: Cascade, 2023. xxii + 227 pages. $32.00.

Catholic social learning remains an underexplored aspect of Catholic social teaching. While Catholic social teaching itself is often referred to as the Church's "best kept secret," Catholic social learning feels even more elusive, like a hidden treasure locked away on a high shelf. This presents a clear paradox: social teaching should not remain theoretical but must be lived out in daily life. In his book, Roger Bergman, long-time director of Creighton University's Justice and Peace Program, not only illustrates how Catholic social learning can be accomplished but also highlights how universities can serve as fertile ground for cultivating social justice. As spaces where we regularly engage others, universities offer opportunities for the personal encounters Bergman sees as "the key to perspective transformation and therefore to an effective justice pedagogy" (11).

Originally published ten years ago, the book has since then been expanded with two new chapters and an afterword by the current director of the Justice and Peace Program, Daniel R. DiLeo. These additions provide spiritual and theological reflections, particularly focusing on the complexities of shame and the enduring belief in God's saving grace, using Job as a moral exemplar. The expanded edition excels in both scholarly depth and pedagogical insight. Bergman navigates complex topics like Aristotle's philosophy of virtue, Alasdair MacIntyre's emphasis on moral inquiry, or St. John Henry Newman's vision of the university, making these ideas accessible while advancing his central concept of promoting justice in the world. His work is deeply grounded in Ignatian pedagogy and the pastoral circle—what Bergman calls the "pedagogical circle" (33)—which he integrates with Joseph Cardijn's see-judge-act method.

Bergman presents three ways his students experience social learning: an immersion experience in Haiti and the Dominican Republic, local service-learning projects, and encountering the lives of moral exemplars. The semester abroad experience offers a profound cultural and spiritual immersion; the drawback is that it is only accessible to a few students. Bergman also reflects on local service-learning programs involving a larger student population. Whether it is serving in soup kitchens, tutoring in underfunded schools, or working with people experiencing homelessness, these experiences foster deep personal reflection, especially when students witness the suffering of their neighbors up close. Additionally, Bergman emphasizes the powers of moral exemplars—such as Dorothy Day, St. Oscar Romero, or Martin Luther King, Jr.—in showing the virtues people may need to acquire as they confront a world "riddled with injustice, violence, and suffering" (115).

Bergman suggests that universities are uniquely positioned to offer these transformational experiences. Drawing on the writings of St. John Henry Newman and St. Ignatius of Loyola, he insists that education is not an end in itself but should be a catalyst to change the world. In this expanded edition, *Catholic Social Learning* remains a crucial resource, especially for educators seeking to integrate Catholic social teaching into people's daily lives and foster the "culture of encounter" for which Pope Francis has been advocating. However, given the evolving landscape of Catholic higher education, it may be time to reconsider the role of Catholic universities as vehicles for change. With many students themselves belonging to vulnerable populations, it is worth exploring how the virtues learned in social justice work might be practiced both within and beyond the university setting.

JENS MUELLER
Notre Dame of Maryland University

A Primer in Christian Ethics: Christ and the Struggle to Live Well. By Luke Bretherton. Cambridge: Cambridge University Press, 2023. vii + 377 pages. $34.99.

The term *primer* can have multiple meanings across varied fields, referring to an introductory text for new students, a guide to a previously unknown domain, a devotional manual, and even (in chemistry) a catalyst for reactions that generate new compounds. Luke Bretherton's aspirations in his new volume incorporate all these valences, though perhaps the last (the laboratory sense) is the most prominent. In the final chapter Bretherton admits, "I am aware that throughout this book I raise more questions than I answer" (360), suggesting that the goal of the book is to use classic concepts from Christian ethics to spur novel kinds of theo-political reflection. In this sense, it follows the lineage of Bretherton's colleague Stanley Hauerwas, whose *The Peaceable Kingdom: A Primer in Christian Ethics* moved well beyond explaining introductory concepts to the task of constructive and controversial ethical analysis.

The similarities between Bretherton's and Hauerwas's approaches extend beyond title and format. Both draw from the deep well of virtue ethics tradition and apply the Christian vision of the good life not only to personal but also political issues. Also like his predecessor, Bretherton refuses to reduce Christian ethics to formulaic casuistry.

This does not mean, however, that Bretherton dodges practical questions by tethering his analysis to the lofty realms of theory alone. His first chapter begins with specific acts of violence (the St. Bartholomew's Day Massacre of 1572 and the mass shooting by Dylann Roof in 2015 at Emmanuel African Methodist Episcopal Church in Charleston, South Carolina), and throughout the book Bretherton grounds all his ethical concepts to precise political and social issues, especially environmental and economic ones. The *cantus firmus* is that humans learn about God and ethics by walking "interlaced pathways" composed of a "meshwork of physical, biotic, social, and spiritual relations" (13), and therefore that all Christian concepts are inseparable from political ramifications. In each chapter Bretherton explores diverse ethical themes by investigating not only their biblical and magisterial origins but also their relatedness to contemporary questions. Striking examples of this novel approach include his "metabolic" analysis of the *imago Dei* concept (32–39), in which he argues that the famed Genesis idea not only tempers the "dominion" of humans over nature, but also the throughput avenues humans occupy within nature.

Another unique contribution that goes beyond most previous ethical primers is the attentiveness to the liberationist tradition of Christian theology, framed as the virtue of "being hospitable to strangers" (91). Bretherton is not the first theologian to link liberation theology to virtue ethics—the tradition of "spiritualities of liberation" found in Gustavo Gutiérrez, James Cone, Roberto Goizueta, and even Martin Luther King, Jr., includes this element, as well—but Bretherton provides an ecological twist that adds a new layer of metaphysical grounding to the relationship between political advocacy and Christian moral formation. Bretherton shows how the organic interconnections between human communities necessitate intentional listening to downplayed voices, as well as critical self-awareness of how often those of us "whose behaviors and bodies comport with what is deemed normal or socially correct feel (our) behaviors are simply good, right, and proper" (92–93). The connection Bretherton forges between liberationist politics and virtue ethics is helpful for addressing the subtle tendency of the latter to reinforce modes of life privileging specific traditions and virtues such as those established by wealthy white men, or westerners in general.

As a textbook, the wide-ranging and practical qualities of Bretherton's book will make it ideal for classroom use. However, although Bretherton's writing is admirably clear and relatively jargon-free, its main drawback is that it regularly alludes to writers and theological paradigms a student would need to understand prior to grasping the main thrust of the work. For example, Bretherton's fascinating exploration of "vocation and neighbor love" (164–171) pulls ideas from Barth, Kierkegaard, and Bonhoeffer in ways that would likely not make sense to a reader unfamiliar with these authors. For this reason, the book might be best used in graduate school and seminary ethics classes, or possibly in advanced undergraduate courses.

From a scholarly angle, this work will prove essential reading for theologians and ethicists interested in finding untrodden common ground between the aretaic tradition and liberation theology. Bretherton's skillful fusing of ancient wisdom with modern ecological and radical political thought will serve as an excellent model for scholars exploring what he calls "God's great economy of creaturely life" (311).

ANDREW BLOSSER
Marquette University

The Eucharistic Vision of Laudato Si'*: Praise, Conversion, and Integral Ecology*. By Lucas Briola. Washington, DC: The Catholic University of America Press, 2023. ix + 277 pages. $34.95.

The ecological crisis that ravages communities, nations, and even individual families presents not only an immediate practical dilemma in how to address issues such as property damage and loss of life for those affected by environmental destruction, but also an existential and theological quandary in how we envision ourselves *vis-à-vis* the rest of creation. In *The Eucharistic Vision of* Laudato Si', Lucas Briola adeptly identifies that, in order for our praxis to change in how we care for and nurture the rest of creation, we must fundamentally provide a robust practical wisdom that seeks the integration of all of creation toward a doxological vision.

Briola argues that the Eucharistic moment serves as a matrix between the healing capacities of God's grace and the creative flourishing of creation's praise, one which should act as locus for the transformation of values for the embodied expression of what Pope Francis describes as "culture of care" (222). Briola develops this argument in light of, first, the pastoral needs arising from the global ecological crisis and, second, the tumultuous reception of Pope Francis's encyclical *Laudato Si'* in his native United States of America. In utilizing Bernard Lonergan's theoretical framework to provide an *explanatory* rather than *descriptive* account of a hoped-for notion of integral ecology (107), Briola outlines categories of thought required to confront the ecological crisis of our times. Briola admits that Lonergan may initially appear inappropriate as interlocutor since he never explicitly wrote on the ecological crisis; however, Briola argues that Lonergan's more comprehensive study of history can assist the body of Christ in constructing an integral ecology necessary for fruitfully interpreting humanity's priestly role in creation, a priestly role that does not envision humanity as in dominion over creation but as leaders existing in the world to orient all of creation in loving praise to the Creator.

While drawing on Lonergan's framework of *progress, decline,* and *redemption* to identify "schemes of recurrence" (115) throughout human action and history, Briola also notably introduces Robert M. Doran's complementary work on the scale of values as a method to advance Eucharistic praise as central to the movements of history. The introduction of Doran's work is extremely beneficial to Briola's overall argument as it aids in promoting an ecology that considers the integral components of all human values and their situatedness in the rest of creation.

Briola's contribution is twofold. Primarily, the insistence on a doxological orientation toward a Eucharistic vision of our common home grounds, in light of the critiques pushed forth by a "technocratic paradigm" (165), a Catholic social teaching within a lived profession of faith. It is a profession of faith that seeks to establish our particularized priestly vocation of stewardship of creation while also universalizing its scope so that "human ecology" is not placed in contrast with, but rather enveloped within, a more expansive "integral ecology." Secondly, Briola's contribution is a welcome addition to the application of Lonergan's thought to research on eco-theology. In introducing Lonergan's categories of *bias*—in all its variances—Briola successfully articulates the need for a more encompassing healing vector in history that seeks creative response through utilizing Lonergan's historical framework of *progress, decline,* and *redemption.*

The theoretical care given to developing a notion of integral ecology, when implemented correctly, should address the pastoral concerns Briola mentions at the root of *Laudato Si*'s mixed reception. While the project does seek to provide a systematic response to the particular reception of *Laudato Si'* in American context, it is fecund in presenting a working theoretical framework in which an intimately doxological perspective may support an integral ecological worldview within the international ecclesial community.

PATRICK NOLIN
Regis St. Michael's Faculty of Theology
University of Toronto

Jesus the Refugee: Ancient Injustice and Modern Solidarity. By D. Glenn Butner, Jr. Minneapolis, MN: Fortress, 2024. xi + 230 pages. $25.00.

In 1952, Pope Pius XII published the apostolic constitution *Exsul Familia Nazarethana*. This constructive and timely document advocated for both sensitive pastoral care and fitting institutional arrangements to alleviate the suffering of migrants. The context of that papal statement included a sharp upsurge in the number of people displaced by widespread turbulence in the wake of the Second World War and the gradual development of institutions (such as the establishment of the United Nations' High Commissioner for Refugees in 1950) and norms (such as the 1951 Refugee Convention) to manage the migration crisis then unfolding in many parts of the world.

Whereas Pius XII appealed to the image of the holy family of Jesus, Mary, and Joseph in their most vulnerable moment as a poignant but brief rhetorical trope, D. Glenn Butner, Jr. dwells on this motif at considerable length—indeed, employing it as the central hinge of this eminently readable volume. The author sets up a revealing thought experiment, asking: Would the holy family be granted refugee status and asylum protection today under contemporary refugee law and prevailing policy regimes? Would their asylum claim not be summarily denied? With ample documentation from numerous relevant disciplines and wide-ranging bodies of literature, Butner explores this central guiding question with great insight on the way to some rather pointed conclusions regarding structural inequities in the treatment of displaced people today.

This volume contributes to a valuable trajectory by which Christian ethicists have been constructing a full-blown Christian theology of migration. Butner does well to draw upon the impressive previous work of such theologians as Kristin Heyer, Miguel De La Torre, and Tisha Rajendra, frequently citing and extending their seminal insights and categories to build the case for recognizing a range of solemn obligations to displaced people. Perhaps the most original contribution of this volume is the highly deliberate effort to clarify the contours of these proposed obligations. While to perceive that "Christians are called to solidarity with refugees in part because Jesus has identified himself with refugees" (132) is straightforward enough, to establish and distinguish various levels of solidarity and responsibility (Butner proposes three categories: universal, particular, and special) and further to advance the claim that these ethical duties apply not just to Christian communities but also to the operations of governments of the pluralistic societies they inhabit requires considerably more effort.

If indeed we will ever succeed in forging widely persuasive justifications for a broader sense of social responsibilities to refugees, Butner's work in this volume points the way and provides a good dose of the content. Mustering a national or even international commitment of resources to protecting and resettling refugees in line with their dignity will likely depend on first coming to terms with the history of systematic disadvantage and global misuse of power (via colonization and economic exploitation) as well as the perduring complicity in ongoing oppression on the part of the inhabitants of privileged nations. Raising awareness of this history of asymmetrical power is a necessary step on the way to fulfilling the "duties of restitution" (155) Butner treats with great insight. The repaying of such debts is not something that can happen only within churches; the most promising initiatives will unfold at the intersection of statecraft, culture, and faith—replete with a political dimension as well as an ecclesiological one.

Among the many merits of this volume is the refreshing and highly accessible writing style of the author, who repeatedly dips into his own personal experience to illustrate vital points. The reader is treated to vivid narratives of Butner's encounters with anti-Hispanic bigotry in the US (189) and the challenges he faced while volunteering to conduct some ESL teaching for a resettled Burmese refugee family (141). We might all benefit from what Butner refers to as "my ongoing awakening to the experiences of refugees and other immigrants and to the need for substantial change in the international refugee regime" (x). None of this, of course, reduces the urgent task of living out an ethic of refugee justice to "being content to feel compassion and to act in small ways" (3), however important that may be; it is also vital to contribute to effecting structural change at every level—local, national, and global.

One might like to see in this work expanded treatment of the sanctuary movement and the efforts of Pope Francis to advocate for solidarity with refugees and migrants, since these both support so clearly the project of this fine volume.

THOMAS MASSARO
Fordham University

Fratelli Tutti: *A Global Commentary.* Edited by William T. Cavanaugh, Carlos Mendoza-Álvarez, OP, Ikenna Ugochukwu Okafor, and Daniel Franklin E. Pilario, CM. Eugene, OR: Cascade, 2024. xxx + 329 pages. $44.00 (paperback).

Fratelli Tutti is rightly considered one of the hidden gems of the papacy of Francis. The relentless pace of news cycles during this highly consequential papacy has exposed us all to a habitual whiplash of overstimulation—a syndrome that may cause us to overlook certain hidden riches. Further, this 2020 social encyclical has regrettably been somewhat "lost in the shuffle" amidst the steady flow of other groundbreaking documents emanating from Rome in recent years. Future generations will surely benefit from our contemporary efforts to raise the profile of *Fratelli Tutti* and prevent its weighty contributions from being eclipsed by other ecclesial developments.

Coming to the rescue is this collection of essays under review. By far the most extensive item of secondary literature on this encyclical currently available in English, this commentary identifies and abundantly illuminates the full range of relevant topics within Francis's text. Indeed, it might be argued that one shortcoming of the encyclical is its compendious nature. In some ways, it emerges more as a resource document on social justice than a tightly focused treatment of any single issue or question. Those looking for guidance on policy issues such as capital punishment or possible justifications for the use of military force may find what they are looking for in the pages of this long document, as would a homilist preparing remarks on the parable of the Good Samaritan. The authors of the insightful and generally well-framed essays within this volume display great skill in preventing "the forest being lost for the trees." The reader is very frequently treated to learned forays into the implications of the moral exhortations Francis proposes regarding political and economic justice in his stirring encyclical.

It is most appropriate that this highly valuable volume appears in the publisher's series Studies in World Catholicism, joining a dozen previous volumes that probe a range of vital ecclesial issues from multiple perspectives that reflect many cultures. The nearly three dozen contributors (many of them quite prominent figures in the global church, including academics and other varieties of ecclesial leaders) offer viewpoints that represent diverse communities in most corners of earth. Each of the four co-editors hails from a different continent and a majority of the essayists represent the Global South. The volume's eight parts correspond to the eight chapters of *Fratelli Tutti*, and each features a mini-chorus of voices treating themes found within the corresponding section of the visionary document of Francis.

Standing out as an especially valuable contribution to theological discourse is part four of the volume (felicitously borrowing Pope Francis's title "A Heart Open to the Whole World"), which provides commentary centered on the implications for the contemporary refugee crisis of *Fratelli Tutti*'s call for universal solidarity. Here, the reader is challenged to consider the many possible obligations that proceed from the Christian commitment to a thoroughly inclusive (even cosmopolitan) vision of the meaning of human community. These several authors call out the toxic xenophobia and extreme nationalism poisoning the prospects for authentic global solidarity, providing a cogent diagnosis of distressing moral deficiencies and resulting social injustices. Besides encapsulating the specific content of the appeal of Pope Francis for greater effort to overcome the tragic global indifference to refugees, these essays make palpable the spirit of Jesus's Parable of the Good Samaritan (the focus of part two of this volume) as it applies especially poignantly to the plight of displaced "people on the move."

As is often the case in ambitious collections of essays, there is a certain unevenness in the quality and originality of the contributions. While a solid majority succeed in braiding together the concerns of local church communities (often explicitly conscious of the aftereffects of the Covid pandemic that weaken constructive social engagement) with the agenda of Francis in the encyclical under consideration, a few stray a bit too far for comfort from the task of engaging the actual message of the pope in *Fratelli Tutti*. Still, the reader is consistently well served by this solidly researched volume for the many insights and creative applications to real-world contexts it brings to bear on the ethical content of this momentous social encyclical.

THOMAS MASSARO
Fordham University

Jewish Virtue Ethics. Edited by Geoffrey D. Claussen, Alexander Green, and Alan L. Mittelman. SUNY Series in Contemporary Jewish Thought. Albany, NY: State University of New York Press, 2023. xii + 519 pages. $39.95.

Noting an "underdeveloped" field in the Jewish tradition, *Jewish Virtue Ethics* surveys Judaism's ongoing interest in character and its excellences. Over thirty-five essays (mostly individual portraits of key thinkers), each contributor addresses four questions: the importance of virtue ethics in the source, the primacy of particular virtues, the specific means of virtue cultivation, and its impact on self-understandings of Judaism and Jewish identity. "Who, then, beyond some in the Jewish community, can Jewish virtue ethics speak to today?" So wonders Alan Mittelman in his epilogue, imagining as fitting interlocutors "communitarians, especially if they are religiously committed" (500).

If communitarians generally are predisposed as dialogue partners, Catholics should be particularly motivated to respond. "Dialogue and friendship with the children of Israel," encourages Pope Francis, "are part of the life of Jesus's disciples" (*Evangelii Gaudium*, no. 248).

Aligned with the Hebrew Bible's abiding concern for what it means to be the People of Israel (B'nai Yisrael), in the first chapter, Amanda Beckenstein Mbuvi outlines how virtue accords with moral paradigms of covenant, priesthood, and family and illustrates their commingling in the curious case of King David. Drawing on the Rabbinic literature, Deborah Baer emphasizes how the tradition distinguishes itself, particularly in the ideal of the righteous sage who embodies Torah for his community. In subsequent chapters on medieval thinkers like Bahya ibn Paquda (1050–1080 CE) to modern ones, readers are offered varying exemplarist approaches (notably, Moses appears in most contributions) and more virtue-focused contributions, tending to prioritize humility and compassion.

Acts of storytelling correct misunderstandings that Jewish ethics hinges entirely on observing the law. A notable example is Sarah Zager's examination of *Or Yisrael* by Rabbi Israel Salanter (1809–1889), as she argues his virtue model both "manipulates tropes" from Jewish discourse and creatively appropriates yet departs from "contemporary Aristotelian virtue theories" (313). For Salanter, the performative and narrative context of "ritualized practice of study" (*limmud musar*) is crucial because the purpose of virtue ethics is primarily about curing spiritual ailments (i.e., vices), and not developing character. Just as one would consult a doctor for an illness, one should consult a "doctor of the soul" (viz., the Torah). By impassioned communal chants (*hitpa'alut*) of sayings about virtues in rabbinic literature, according to Zager, students may foster proper fear of God and facilitate an "emotional release" (317) that rectifies any inclinations to evil.

The volume avails resources to navigate and reinterpret complicated relations between law and virtue cultivation. For Nahmanides (affectionately called Ramban, 1194–1270 CE), Jonathan Jacobs observes, the law is a necessary guide for instructing right relations, and yet also inherently indicates the need "to go beyond the letter of law." In his comment on the general commandment to "do what is right and good" (Deut 6:18), for instance, Ramban addresses the goal of justice in the marketplace but also beyond "so that one is known as someone of honesty and integrity in every aspect of behavior" (130–131). In the virtue jurisprudence of Rabbi Joseph Soloveitchik (1903–1993), on the other hand, the law is framed as a "discipline" (*musar*) that yields its own distinct virtues and dispositions (420). Alternatively, as found in the *Iggerot Ha-Ra'ayyah* by Rabbi Abraham Isaac Kook (1863–1935), Don Seeman reflects how "reasons for the commandments" (*ta'amei ha-mitzvot*) become clarified once agency becomes aligned with divine purposes, writing, "correct proportion between virtue's freedom and law's obligation, Kook once observed, is like the proportion between the scaffolding of a building (law) and the open space in which human activity transpires (virtue)" (362).

Other contributions will surprise readers in encountering familiar thinkers anew. Although Martin Buber (1878–1965) is rarely read as a virtue ethicist, William Plevan notes Buber's overall concern with perfection as "the self-actualization of each human being's unique personality" (370) and names accordingly openness and dialogical responsiveness as key dispositions in that pursuit. Buber's notion of dialogue can also be founded in ways humanity is drawn into imitation of "divine *middot*, or attributes, of clothing the naked, visiting the sick, comforting mourners, and burying the dead" (378).

Similarly fruitful, Ned Curthoys situates the works of Hannah Arendt (1906–1975) in the Jewish "pariah tradition." It is well known that Arendt endeavored to elaborate how the pursuit of excellence involves skills of practical reasoning and intellectual virtues to aid conscience's capacity to judge, deliberate, and act. Retrieving Aristotle, furthermore, her conception of the good life is formulated in terms of human dignity and self-care, not selflessness. As an outsider who resists anti-Semitism and all forms of dehumanization, Curthoys poignantly stresses Arendt's admiration for Socrates as "*the* exemplary philosopher, a courageous, dialogically motivated, and publicly engaged intellectual remembered for his close friendships" (428). In a particularly Jewish way, Curthoys's Arendt accordingly employs the "critical perspective of the outsider among one's people and rebels against injustices inflicted on oppressed people more generally" (436).

At times, the experience of reading this book is like digesting an annotated anthology. Ultimately, however, it lends itself well to precisely what is identified as the basic goal of Jewish-Christian dialogue by the Commission for Religious Relations with the Jews: "One can only learn to love what one has gradually come to know, and one can only know truly and profoundly what one loves" (no. 44). Indeed, that learning is best done in dialogue and friendship. For moral theology, at the very least, this book signifies an invitation to a gradual deepening and possibly the mutual enrichment between our virtue traditions.

MICHAEL VANZANDT COLLINS
Assumption University (Windsor, ON)

The Catholic Case Against War: A Brief Guide. By David Carroll Cochran. Notre Dame, IN: University of Notre Dame Press, 2024. ix + 182 pages. $32.00 (paperback).

With this volume David Carroll Cochran has done a service for Catholics and others interested in a faith-based appraisal of war by laying out a focused exploration of the church's teaching about the failures of the resort to war. The author guides readers through a largely socio-political exploration of the church's critical stance toward the contemporary waging of war. For Catholics, people of other faiths, and all those of good will, Cochran focuses the conversation on the moral illegitimacy and evils of war. He directs our attention to war's lies, destruction, and dehumanizing consequences, and points toward available alternatives to armed conflict.

The author notes that his purposes are to draw together Vatican documents that comprise the church's case against war itself, and to showcase the practicality of this case. Chapters 1 and 2 lay out an analysis of the false promises and death which attend war. Chapters 3 through 5 describe political and economic strategies for preventing and even abolishing war.

One of the strengths of the book is that Cochran pulls together stimulating research in a readable and teachable form, drawing on examples from around the world and multiple conflicts, including both world wars, Iraq, Libya, and Vietnam. Each chapter starts by highlighting church teachings, then turns to other sources to provide political, economic, legal, and historical analysis.

Cochran delivers a powerful reading of papal condemnations of suffering caused by war and preparation for war, the destruction of morality, and the dehumanization of all touched by armed conflict. He notes that the waging of war engenders a dangerous epistemology with false promises of war's governability, guarantees of success, the nobility of "our side," and the safeguarding of justice. Rather, war provokes future wars, violence, destruction, and deception. In chapter 2, the author argues that the renunciation of violence bears witness to the truth, and he provides illustrative examples of nonviolent civil resistance—in places such as Belarus, India, Iran, the Philippines, Poland, South Africa, and Thailand—while recognizing varying degrees of "success" in these nonviolent efforts to resolve large-scale violence.

Cochran highlights strategies for promoting solidarity, mutual aid, and dialogue in the political, legal, and economic domains, with the likelihood of preventing particular wars from starting. Efforts within individual countries around the globe can build structures of peace and promote virtues that stand against a reflexive recourse to warmaking. The author acknowledges that these efforts reflect a long perspective, yet there is always something to be done right now.

The book implicitly reasons from a Catholic social teaching framework that the Catholic case against war is focused on transforming social structures, including on a global level, to make the outbreak of war less likely. We read in chapter 5 an argument that, just as once widely accepted practices of institutionalized violence (including the death penalty, trial by combat, duels, and chattel slavery) were largely eliminated, so too a world without war is better than one with it. He further makes the point that this condition is possible, if not entirely probable. A helpful component of Cochran's analysis is his clarification of what a world without war does *not* mean. It would not mean an end to injustice, political violence, or national greed.

The list of texts provided as Recommended Reading, as well as in the Notes, Works Cited, and Index, are invaluable for the reader interested in learning more. The list of Vatican documents and papal statements is especially useful. Other cited texts are drawn from the works of multiple scholars, largely though not exclusively from the 2000s.

I highly recommend study of this book. Cochran provides a good primer with a political focus. The text is a good fit for undergraduate and graduate college courses, as well as parish reading groups and adult faith formation. The title might have been a bit sharper, perhaps along the lines of 'The Contemporary Catholic Socio-Political Case Against War.' In addition to politics, we can point to other sympathetic arguments from the church for peacemaking and against war, such as the World Day of Peace Messages from Pope Francis which emphasize cultivating fraternity, engaging in practices of dialogue, and building a culture of solidarity and mercy. A whole series of guides of similar length and structure but with different starting points, such as the abolition of war and promotion of peace in relation to the sacraments and liturgical participation or to an understanding of the church as a pilgrim people of hope, would be another wonderful resource for teachers and catechists. Right now, though, we can read and study this book with others and follow along where it brings us.

MARC TUMEINSKI
Anna Maria College

Parenting: The Complex and Beautiful Vocation of Raising Children. By Holly Taylor Coolman. Grand Rapids, MI: Baker Academic, 2024. xv + 144 pages. $21.99.

The last several decades have seen a dramatic change in the field of moral theology as the percentage of specialists became predominantly lay. Thus, many moral theologians have first-hand experience in an area of crucial ecclesiological and moral importance: parenting. Duties and failures of parents are not exactly a new topic in moral theology, nor is the notion of the family as domestic church.

And popular parenting books abound, focusing on themes from sleep to spiritual advice.

Yet Holly Taylor Coolman's book represents something a bit different, rooted firmly in both the author's experience as a parent and her expertise as a theologian. The format and style of the book, including minimal endnotes and a helpful "Suggested Reading" section, makes this manuscript accessible—and helpful—to non-academics of any Christian denomination. Her insights also are worthy of the attention of moral theologians; parenting is a significant ethical topic.

The author's structure might be considered roughly chronological through the life of a child and the parent's experiences: infancy, toddler, the growing years, adolescence, later adolescence, and into adulthood, including supporting an adult child who is married. Nestled within this chronological structure are topical chapters such as discipline, new technology, survival mode, busy days, single parents, and school. Of note is her conception of parenting viewed as "mapmaking" or "apprenticeship," parents leading and guiding in a companionable way rather than authoritarian (chapter 5). These approaches seem both practical and rooted in Christian faith.

Coolman's particular insight as an adoptive parent adds richness to her account, as seen particularly in chapter 2, "Beyond Birth: Other Ways of Welcoming Children." The book invites the reader to consider hospitality as a theme of parenting, including acknowledging loss and "making space" for feelings of grief. The additional demands of foster parenting or adoptive parenting require greater understanding and support from the community. Reading Coolman, one wonders if the usual normalizing of the biological, nuclear family has left us with a theologically impoverished view of family life.

Recent moral theology has shown us the importance of the social aspect of ethics, and Coolman rightly emphasizes that "parents who build a family are also building a community" rooted in the community of the church, with Christ as the head (17). The circumstances of industrialization and the nuclear family can be isolating to parents, and this can be devastating to their work as parents. Thus, the author highlights the importance of parents finding a good support network and provides excellent practical ideas for others, including churches, to support parents.

The theme of community stretches throughout the book in a unifying manner, and this emphasis on the social and communal aspect of parenting may be one of the book's greatest strengths. We can see the ideal and how crucial support is for parents, whether in crisis or in everyday life. Having a strong network allows parents and children to thrive.

However, a potential pitfall of Coolman's emphasis is community becoming another obligation for already overburdened parents. They may find themselves in circumstances where, despite efforts, they simply cannot get the help they need or find a supportive network that facilitates flourishing. Parents may choose, at great financial sacrifice, to move to a seemingly great community, only to find that this community has a multitude of problems that compromise, rather than further, the integrity of their family. Unfortunately, parents may work hard to contribute to a church community, only to find nothing reciprocated in their times of need. Especially in our modern circumstances, failure to find or participate in a strong community should not lead parents to feel like they themselves are failures.

Instead, this particular imperfect situation can be viewed positively, like other challenges, when it is an occasion for uniting struggles to the cross; moving forward means embracing suffering, including the feelings of isolation that may occur. The Catholic practice of embracing the "death to self" of mortification would be one way to expand on Coolman's work.

Also related, the reader could benefit from Coolman exploring the suffering of parents in a supernatural context, with support not only from the visible church community, but the larger mystical body including the angels and saints, with reliance on the sacraments. The grace of the sacrament of marriage is an important starting point for family life. When parents feel overcome with their own failures, they can turn to forgiveness in the sacrament of confession and try again. Further, when parents cannot find the support they need from a community, they can receive strength and comfort from the Eucharist.

There are advantages to Coolman's book being accessible to any Christian denomination, nor does this preclude relevance to Catholic moral theology. Yet we also see an opportunity for Coolman and other authors writing in this field to think further on topics of parenting.

MARIA C. MORROW
Independent Scholar

Finding Faith in Business: An Economy of Communion Vision. Edited by Andrew Gustafson and Celeste Harvey. Hyde Park, NY: New City, 2024. 300 pages. $25.95.

The last word of the subtitle of this book speaks to what it is fundamentally about: a different *vision* of economic and business life. The Economy of Communion (EoC) is an association of enterprises, now around 850 worldwide, born of the Focolare movement. As Focolare founder Chiara Lubich remarked in a 1999 address, reproduced as chapter 3, the EoC began in Brazil in 1991 in response to the realization that "we [Focolare] were unable to cover even the most urgent needs of our members, notwithstanding the intense communion of goods" (41). So members started businesses. As Andrew Gustafson and Celeste Harvey note in the introduction, there came to be three recognized purposes for profit: "(1) direct assistance to the poor, (2) promotion of a culture of giving, and (3) re-investment in the business" (19). Maximizing profit for the owners is not part of the equation. The purpose of an EoC business is to build up community.

The book consists of three parts: first, three introductory chapters, including a 2017 address by Pope Francis to an EoC meeting, as well as the chapters by Gustafson and Harvey, and Lubich; second, four chapters under the heading of "Practice"; and third, six chapters under the heading of "Theory." As with most collections, the chapters vary in quality, and there is more than a little repetition. Excluding the addresses by Pope Francis and Lubich, the chapters originated as papers presented at a conference held at Creighton University in 2018. Some chapters retain traces of that origin: there is a reference to "this roundtable" (152), and an event fatefully scheduled for March 2020 is mentioned in the future tense (156). Surprisingly, there are very few examples of EoC businesses discussed at any length, which would have strengthened the book. The major exception is Andrew Gustafson's excellent chapter, "The Economy of Communion: Catholic Social Thought Put to Work," in which he discusses his business of buying and renovating old houses in Omaha, Nebraska, which he then rents at below-market rates. Gustafson is honest about the challenges of "making decisions which lead to more communion but don't always lead to the most efficient bottom line" (137). He also makes plain, though, the personal and even spiritual benefits of operating "relationally, not transactionally" (128), and to that end rejecting the idolatry of profit as "the ultimate justification" (127).

Celeste Harvey's chapter, "A Person-Centered Theory of the Firm," helpfully situates the EoC among other "contemporary movements seeking to re-envision business as a force for good," such as the B Corps movement and social entrepreneurship (190). On her account, EoC enterprises make a special contribution to imagining "the possibility for persons of conscience and good will to be fully invested in the realm of business without bifurcation into a 'private' self and a 'business self'" (217). That note is likewise sounded in Gustafson's chapter. For an EoC-inspired entrepreneur like himself, business relations are not distinct from "normal human relations"; to the contrary, "business is in fact fundamentally human interaction revolving around meeting personal human needs and wants" (123). David Cloutier's chapter, "Simplicity of Lifestyle as a Goal of Business," introduces the Italian economist Stefano Zamagni's work on the "civil economy," picturing the *telos* of economic activity to be service to the common good and which Zamagni sees the EoC as reviving after centuries of domination by profit-driven capitalism. According to Cloutier, the model of the economy the EoC rejects is what Pope Benedict XVI called the "market-plus-state binary," which pictures business as "for pursuing private goods, while government is for pursuing common goods" through taxation and re-distribution of earnings (76). By contrast, EoC enterprises seek to observe what has come to be called *pre*-distributive justice, practicing business in such a way that it reinforces social ties rather than undermining them and thereby requiring repair by the state (77).

As Jeanne Buckeye notes in her chapter, "Exploring Subsidiarity," the EoC is still "relatively unknown" in the business world (259). It seems fair to wonder, then, just how likely the EoC is to achieve what Buckeye describes as its goal: namely, to establish "a new kind of economic culture where building community and sharing abundance with the poor take precedence over market dominance and the accumulation of wealth" (259). That said, there is undeniably a growing thirst to do business differently, and as Pope Francis beautifully remarked in his 2017 address, "The changes in the order of the spirit and therefore of life are not linked to big numbers. The small flock, the lamp, a coin, a lamb, a pearl, salt, leaven: these are the images of the Kingdom that we encounter in the Gospels" (37). This book makes a plausible case that the EoC, too, may be considered an image of the Kingdom.

BERNARD G. PRUSAK
John Carroll University

All Oppression Shall Cease: A History of Slavery, Abolitionism, and the Catholic Church. By Christopher J. Kellerman, SJ. Maryknoll, NY: Orbis Books, 2022. xviii + 230 pages. $26.00.

This is a most praiseworthy book for its coverage of a largely ignored yet significant question: What did the Catholic Church teach and practice regarding enslaving human beings? It gathers historical facts—little known or largely misunderstood—to describe and critique the church's history of theological teachings and practices regarding slaveholding, beginning with the Scriptures up to the contemporary Catholic social teaching tradition. As a Jamaican Catholic woman, descended from enslaved Africans, I found this a bittersweet read, as I was forced to confront the all too human contradictions of individual Catholics, priests, popes, and councils from the time of the early church up to today. I was forced to face the cruelty and moral turpitude of individual Catholics, priests, and popes, who dared to buy, sell, and abuse human beings, fully sanctioned by canon law, Roman law, church councils, Fathers and Doctors of the church, theologians, popes, and the Roman Curia. Sadly, I can never look at Peter Claver the same again. The truth of his participation in the trafficking and enslaving of Africans must be told across the Caribbean, where a false picture continues to be painted and his name immortalized on many an ecclesial building!

Kellerman's argument across ten chapters has a powerful refrain—"slaveholding is a choice"—that takes various forms: "As common as slaveholding may have been among Catholic religious orders, it was always a choice" (136). He rejects as demonstrably false the argument that "nobody thought it was wrong back then" by introducing myriad voices, including those of the enslaved and formerly enslaved, Black Catholic confraternities, theologians, and laymen. Kellerman is particularly pointed in his critique of the papacy and other religious authorities for their complicity in the enslavement of Africans and their descendants.

In chapter 10, we see the church finally reversing course and condemning slavery under Leo XIII (1888) and his successors. Notably, Kellerman argues cogently that it would be difficult to see the tradition of Catholic social teaching emerging "without first condemning the purchase, domination, and forced labor of another human being. Likewise, how could the gospel of life, so treasured by John Paul II, have been promoted if babies and young children could still be considered property to be bought and sold to the highest bidder on the auction block?" (191). Even so, Leo's successors continued to retell a version of history that ignored the church's slaveholding, endorsement of the transatlantic trade, and allowing the enslaving of descendants of the trafficked Africans for centuries. There is, therefore, a corporate responsibility of confession, penance, restitution, reparations, and amendment the church must face. Even in forcing us to face the horrors of a long-recalcitrant slaveholding Catholic Church, Kellerman exhorts us not to lose hope: "The truth might not always be thriving in the places where we have been trained to look for it. And so, we must listen and be attentive, and we must prayerfully consider what we see and hear" (215).

Abolitionist women are a fleeting presence in the text, with early mentions of Quakers Lucretia Mott and Sarah Grimké, as well as freeborn Maria W. Stewart. Of Catholic abolitionist women, there was only Mary Louise Booth, "a skilled translator, writer, and white Catholic who was also an ardent abolitionist" (163). There is room for further investigation of women's voice and presence across the story of the Catholic Church and abolitionism.

The recommendations for further reading contained only one book by a Caribbean scholar—H. Orlando Patterson—in the general section. A small glimpse of a Catholic abolitionist in the English-speaking Caribbean appears in the brief reference to Dublin-born Richard Madden, a medical doctor in Jamaica and Cuba (chap. 9). Given that the Caribbean was a singular region shaped by the impact of enslavement and the church, it would have been important to point to readings about and from that region. For example, Maureen Warner-Lewis reconstructed a biography of the enslaved African Archibald Monteath (née Aniaso), an Igbo who was kidnapped and trafficked to Jamaica around 1802. He became active in the Moravian Church, later purchasing his freedom. His dedication to the Christian faith made him special to the missionaries and enslaved people alike. B. W. Higman has studied the life and thought of pro-slavery Scottish Anglican priest John Lindsay (1729–1788), whose unpublished work presented a theological justification for the enslavement of Africans along similar lines to Catholics of that period. Andrew Dial published an article on the Jesuit Antoine Lavalette, who tortured to death four enslaved persons in Martinique. Kellerman's research points to the need for a similar monograph on the nature of the theological and practical impact of the Catholic Church's responses to slaveholding in the Caribbean.

ANNA KASAFI PERKINS
University of the West Indies and
St. Michael's Theological College, Jamaica

Justice After War: Jus Post Bellum *in the 21st Century.* By David Chiwon Kwon. Washington, DC: Catholic University of America Press, 2023. xviii + 294 pages. $29.95.

Over the last three decades, scholars, policymakers, and practitioners working within the just war tradition have increasingly gravitated to the concept of *jus post bellum:* "justice after war." Proponents of *"jpb"* (a now standard shorthand) claim it is a necessary supplement to the more familiar just war categories of *jus ad bellum* and *jus in bello.* Whereas *jus ad bellum* concerns the causes of war, and *jus in bello* the means employed in warfare, *jpb* provides moral guidelines for the aftermath of war. What do victors owe the vanquished, and vice versa? What does a just postwar settlement look like? Do non-belligerent actors—civil society groups, or international NGOs—have a necessary role to play? These are central questions in the growing field of *jpb.* But while their urgency is obvious, their answers remain highly disputed.

In this context, David Chiwon Kwon's *Justice After War* is a most welcome contribution. A Catholic moral theologian, Kwon does not confine himself to his own discipline, but aims to offer a comparative analysis of how *jpb* has developed across "moral philosophy, moral theology, security studies, international law, and peacebuilding work" (3). Simultaneously, he seeks to justify *jpb* as a legitimate addition to the just war tradition and advance a constructive argument about what it comprises. Challenging the prevalent view that "political reconciliation" should be the primary objective of postwar reconstruction, Kwon contends that *jpb* ought instead to focus on "human security," and identifies "just policing," "just punishment," and "just political participation" as its three primary elements (3).

Kwon's constructive argument is, in my view, the most original and compelling aspect of *Justice After War*. The book mounts a forceful critique of "maximalist" approaches to *jpb* that expect too much from postwar actors, while failing "to fully examine the essential features of human reality in postwar societies" (70)—in particular, the limitations of time, resources, and human moral agency that constrain what is possible after war. Kwon advocates instead a "maxim(um) of ethical minimalism" that takes these limitations more seriously, and "aims to restrict what just actors ought to do" (148). He also presses for distinguishing the more limited obligations of postwar justice, and the field of *jpb* itself, from the broader and longer-term projects of "transitional justice" (157) and "peacebuilding" (232), often conflated with *jpb*.

There is much to be said for Kwon's argument. Conceptually, narrowing the scope of *jpb* as he suggests offers a much clearer delineation of the field and the problems that define it. Substantively, Kwon's case for greater realism, and less idealism, in *jpb* is persuasive. It rests not only on political pragmatism, but on deeper moral and theological grounds: in particular, the Thomistic tradition of common good ethics (Kwon's principal framework) and the Christian realism of Reinhold Niebuhr, which Kwon synthesizes creatively, if not (as he admits) wholly consistently (266). In the book's final three chapters, Kwon utilizes this ethical framework and draws on a range of interdisciplinary literature to flesh out what his realist conception of *jpb* would involve in practice. His proposals exemplify the Thomistic prudence he advocates.

Not every aspect of *Justice After War* is equally successful. The book's opening engagement with four "foundational" just war theorists (Aristotle, Aquinas, Michael Walzer, and Brian Orend) is too narrow in scope and idiosyncratic in selection to fully situate Kwon's argument, and the category of *jpb* itself, in the broader tradition. Conversely, Kwon scarcely engages critiques of the just war tradition as a whole. Moreover, while Kwon's engagements with non-theological disciplines add important support to his constructive argument, they seem too limited to provide a true comparative analysis of how *jpb* has developed in these fields, as against moral theology. This is partially because Kwon proceeds in dialogue with individual thinkers rather than surveying each field more systematically, a methodological choice that also makes it challenging, at times, to track all the threads in his complex argument. For these reasons, I believe other works might provide a better orientation for students new to the field of just war.

On the other hand, for readers already somewhat versed in Kwon's subject, his book has much to offer. Its interdisciplinary breadth, theological depth, and prudent realism genuinely advance the argument about *jpb*, and yield a plausible vision of what "justice after war" might look like.

NICHOLAS HAYES-MOTA
Santa Clara University

A Christian and African Ethic of Women's Political Participation: Living as Risen Beings. By Léocadie W. Lushombo. Lanham, MD: Lexington, 2023. xvi + 292 pages. $116.00 (hardcover), $45.00 (e-book).

In an era when gender inequality in politics remains a pressing issue, Léocadie W. Lushombo's book offers a critical examination of this multifaceted problem. Her book centers around both African and Christian ethical frameworks, and how their intersection can encourage African women to participate more in political spaces; she maintains a consistent thread throughout the book, arguing that ethical reform is necessary at both theological and cultural levels to achieve genuine gender equality, largely drawing on insights from the Circle of Concerned African Women Theologians, postcolonial critiques, feminist ethics, inculturation theories, liberation theology, and Catholic social teaching.

A notable aspect of Lushombo's work is her ability to combine African and Christian feminist perspectives, which proves her work to be not only a powerful reminder of the patriarchal systems that limit women's voices and agency in Africa, but also solid interdisciplinary scholarship that dives deep into connections between gender dynamics, cultural traditions, and theological imperatives in shaping women's political engagement. This book is broken up into four parts. In the first two parts, Lushombo delves into the issue of "anthropological poverty" and how African Traditional Religion(s) or ATR often overlooks the impoverishment of women. Central to her concerns is anthropological poverty among African women, a concept she adopts from Engelbert Mveng. The term captures a profound loss of identity and dignity stemming from historical traumas such as slavery and colonialism, which continue to be reinforced by ongoing cultural and religious oppression, as shown by the elements of ATR where she carefully examines the barriers that inhibit women from political decision-making processes (64–74). It denies women belief in their ability to participate in human endeavors, create a better life, and prosper (170).

Lushombo shines a bright light on these major challenges and pushes for real change; in the last two parts, she proposes an integrated Chrisitan and African ethic that challenges existing norms and presents a pathway toward empowerment for women. Despite the ways in which both have been used to shape women into the patriarchal roles they currently play, Lushombo offers that African mythology which tells stories of women in power, as well as the Christian concept of a "discipleship of equals" could be used to create a multifaceted approach to increasing women's political participation in Africa. In chapter 7, she explains how patriarchal interpretations of religious texts reinforce gender inequalities by pushing the idea that women should stick to domestic roles which limit their involvement in political life. Lushombo not only points out a significant barrier to women's political participation but also suggests practical steps to overcome it; she stresses the need for educational programs and workshops that teach people about gender equality in religious contexts. Her analysis is backed by concrete examples and personal stories, making her argument both compelling and relatable.

Another crucial topic Lushombo discusses is the economic barriers that prevent women from participating in politics. In chapter 8, she examines how financial constraints and economic dependence significantly limit women's ability to engage in political activities. To address these barriers, she suggests implementing policies that provide financial support and resources for women who would want to enter politics. Finally, the concluding chapter highlights the importance of building solidarity among women and forming networks that can support their political aspirations. She believes that collective action and mutual support can amplify women's voices and enhance their political influence (187).

Lushombo's analysis demonstrates several key strengths. Her focus on structural reforms and cultural transformation reflects a deep understanding of the multifaceted nature of gender inequality. She does not merely call for increased representation of women but advocates for systemic changes that address the root causes of exclusion, such as deeply ingrained patriarchal norms. Her proposals for reinterpreting religious texts and reframing cultural narratives to support gender equality show a strategic approach to overcoming societal norms passed down through generations. The ultimate strength of Lushombo's work lies in her comprehensive and integrative approach, especially the in-depth examination of African traditions and their potential to empower women. She provides a new, intersectional way of interpreting religious texts and appreciating African culture which I believe is constructed to appeal largely to the group they are meant to liberate, something often overlooked by theologians and ethicists. Further, her use of multiple sacred texts, mythologies, and cultural traditions, along with her critical skepticism toward the function of narratives in society, provides a unique theological perspective—not to mention that her engagement with postcolonial theory and narrative criticism provides a robust framework for understanding and addressing the complexities of gender, culture, and politics in Africa. Multifaceted, diverse, equitable programs for reform like Lushombo's seem to be one of the only ways to ensure that a society uplifts all its members.

DAVID KWON
Seattle University

The Personalism of Edith Stein: A Synthesis of Thomism and Phenomenology. By Robert McNamara. Washington, DC: CUA Press, 2023. vii + 297 pages. $75.00.

One might wonder what a review for a book on the metaphysical differences and similarities between Edith Stein and Thomas Aquinas is doing in the *Journal of Moral Theology.* What, after all, do such seemingly esoteric ontological and phenomenological debates have to do with theological ethics or the moral life, with contemporary moral theological discourse and scholarship? Quite a lot, it turns out!

In *The Personalism of Edith Stein: A Synthesis of Thomism and Phenomenology*, Robert McNamara argues: "Stein's engagement with Aquinas represents a fundamental 'personalization' of Thomistic anthropology, a personalization that is worked out differently in [the areas of human nature, human individuality, and the human relation to God]" (248). According to McNamara, "Stein mounts an increasingly compelling case that the personal I is indeed the predominating formative feature in the structure of human nature, and she thus reconsiders all received teachings by passing them through this personalizing lens" (258). Given the Second Vatican Council's call for a more person-centered moral theology, the post-conciliar turn to Thomistic virtue theory and natural law as well as Pope Francis's recent teachings in *Dilexit Nos* on the heart as the core of the person in her unique identity, Stein's phenomenological innovations and "rereading of Thomistic anthropology" are deeply relevant to contemporary discourse in Catholic moral theology (259).

For this reason, Stein's personalism has the potential to act as a bridge in moral methodological debates and bring a richer clarity to the continuity of post-conciliar pontificates. *The Personalism of Edith*

Stein is thus not only a profound contribution to Stein scholarship but to Catholic moral theology and theological ethics in general. This work, although technical and scholarly, is accessible to non-Stein experts and graduate students. McNamara includes his "Prolegomenon: A Preparatory Analysis" at the beginning of the work prior to entering into the substance of the text. This prolegomenon serves as a helpful philosophical grounding. It gives readers who are new to Stein's thought some sturdy scaffolding on which to hang McNamara's subsequent argument. As such, this chapter would act as a good, short philosophical introduction to Stein for a seminar. Although some Stein scholars, like myself, might not fully agree with all of McNamara's descriptions or interpretations of her thought—his choice at times to modify the word "experience" with the term "conscious" comes to mind—this work, nonetheless, gives the reader a clear, robust, and compelling portrait of Stein's philosophy and theological anthropology.

The Personalism of Edith Stein is divided into three parts: (I) Human Nature, (II) The Human Individual, and (III) The Human Being's Relation to God. Each part is composed of two chapters. The first chapter, "Point of Departure in the 'Life of the I,'" discusses how Stein's philosophical starting point of the human person uniquely shapes her thought. It evaluates the extent to which Stein's personalist understanding of the structure of the human person is ultimately consistent with the traditional Thomistic conception of a person as a substance of a rational nature. The second chapter, "Human Unity and Bodily Formation," investigates Stein's conception of the unity and constitution of the human person through the spiritual soul and the extent to which this differs from the Thomistic conception of the rational soul. The third chapter, "The Material Individual," sets out Stein's critique of Thomas's conception of material individuation, explaining her conception of form as the source of individuality. The fourth chapter, "The Human Individual in Particular," goes on to explain Stein's conception of human individuality and personal being given her alternative conception of individuation. The fifth chapter, "Philosophical Knowledge of God," discusses Thomas's analogy of being and Stein's assessment of it. The sixth chapter, "The Personal Form of the Analogy of Being," gives Stein's positive personalist account of the analogy of being, wherein "divine simplicity is best understood from the perspective of the personal 'I am'" (255).

To the great benefit of the reader, each chapter concludes with an assessment of one of Stein's original contributions: (1) the personal "I" as bearer, (2) the spiritual soul as substantial unifier of human nature, (3) individuation, (4) personal, individual human being, (5) the problem of the proportion of essence to being, and (6) the cataphatic, personal analogy of being. Towards the end of the book, McNamara notes, in an insightful act of summation, that in Stein's personalism, "not only does the objective structure of human nature recapitulate the whole of the hierarchically ordered cosmos but each human individual has the potential to progressively encompass the whole of the created cosmos . . . as a finite personal representative of the divine in the created cosmos, a finite personal analogue of the infinite personal Creator" (259).

CATHERINE MOON
Institute for Advanced Studies in Culture
University of Virginia

Perspectives on Psychic Conversion. Edited by Joseph Ogbonnaya. Milwaukee, WI: Marquette University Press, 2023. xxvi + 378 pages. $29.00.

Joseph Ogbonnaya's edited volume *Perspectives on Psychic Conversion* offers a rich and multifaceted exploration of the concept of psychic conversion, building on Bernard Lonergan's triad of intellectual, moral, and religious conversions. The collection of seventeen essays provides a comprehensive examination of the role and implications of psychic conversion across various fields, making it a pivotal read for scholars and practitioners interested in theology, psychology, and social transformation.

The volume is divided into four parts, each addressing different dimensions and applications of psychic conversion. Part one lays the theoretical groundwork, with M. Shawn Copeland's opening chapter highlighting the potential of psychic conversion as a therapeutic tool for addressing social biases and injustices, particularly those related to race and gender in American society. Copeland's engagement with Kelly Brown Douglas's work on Black bodies and justice provides a compelling case for the necessity of integrating psychic conversion into social transformation efforts.

Joseph Ogbonnaya's own contribution in chapter 2 underscores the indispensability of Robert Doran's functional specialties for accessing Lonergan's cognitional theory and existential conversion. Ogbonnaya argues that recognizing the intrinsic connection between the psyche and the mind is crucial for a holistic understanding of meaning and value. This recognition complements Lonergan's intentionality analysis, bridging the gap left by his earlier work.

In chapter 3, John Dadosky further connects Lonergan's ideas to psychology, arguing for the legitimacy and necessity of Doran's concept of psychic conversion. Dadosky asserts that this fourth level of conversion finds its basis in Lonergan's discussions of affective conversion, making a strong case for its integration into contemporary theological discourse.

Mary Josephine MacDonald's chapter 4 brings a creative theological anthropology into dialogue with neuroplasticity and psychology, responding to Lonergan's call for interdisciplinary collaboration. This chapter exemplifies how scientific insights can enrich theological understanding and practice.

Part two delves into the developments in understanding psychic conversion, particularly in relation to bias and attentiveness. Blaise Murray's exploration of bias and bigotry as impediments to human development is notable for its emphasis on the need for psychic conversion to overcome these barriers. Jonathan Heaps and Ryan Hemmer contribute to this discussion by examining terminological allergies and the role of the psyche in speculative method, respectively, each emphasizing the restorative power of psychic conversion.

In part three, the application of psychic conversion to spirituality and trauma is explored. Danielle Nussberger's chapter on spiritual direction employs the RAIN technique to facilitate psychic conversion, fostering communal and social transformation. Joseph K. Gordon's examination of biblical imagery and Gerard Whelan's insights into the Ignatian *Spiritual Exercises* further illustrate the transformative potential of psychic conversion in spiritual contexts.

Randy Rosenberg's discussion of trauma emphasizes the necessity of attending to the neural and psychic dimensions of human experience for healing and self-transcendence. His engagement with the works of Bessel van der Kolk and René Girard enriches the understanding of psychic conversion's role in addressing trauma.

Part four addresses contemporary issues such as racism, decolonization, and education. Cyril Orji's chapter on Replacement Theory and Jeremy Blackwood's exploration of antiblackness demonstrate how psychic conversion can address deep-seated societal biases. Mark Obeten's analysis of decolonization and Andrea Stapleton's evaluation of Catholic higher education highlight the importance of psychic conversion in promoting authentic development and self-transcendence in diverse contexts.

Perspectives on Psychic Conversion is a testament to the impact psychic conversion can have at both individual and societal levels. By situating psychic conversion within the broader framework of Bernard Lonergan's threefold process of intellectual, moral, and religious conversion, this collection not only expands the theoretical discourse but also provides practical insights for addressing contemporary challenges.

For scholars of theology, Ogbonnaya's volume is particularly valuable. The essays offer explorations into how psychic conversion intersects with theological concepts and practices, making it a significant addition to contemporary theological studies. The book's engagement with Lonergan's work and its extension through Doran's contributions provide a theoretical framework that can enhance scholarly understanding and teaching of conversion processes. Psychologists and practitioners in related fields will find the interdisciplinary approach of this volume enlightening. The incorporation of psychological theories, such as neuroplasticity and Jungian psychology, into the discourse on psychic conversion highlights the relevance of this concept for understanding human behavior and mental processes. This makes the book a useful resource for those looking to integrate theological insights with psychological practices, particularly in the context of healing and personal development.

Overall, *Perspectives on Psychic Conversion* stands out as an invaluable resource that bridges theology, psychology, and social ethics. Its interdisciplinary approach and diverse applications make it a crucial text for anyone interested in the multifaceted nature of conversion and its implications for both personal and societal well-being. By addressing contemporary issues through the lens of psychic conversion, Ogbonnaya's volume offers a comprehensive and practical guide for scholars, practitioners, and educators alike.

STEVEN UMBRELLO
University of Turin

On Helping One's Neighbor: Severe Poverty and the Religious Ethics of Obligation. By Bharat Ranganathan. New York: Cambridge University Press, 2024. xxvi + 204 pages. $110.00.

Jesus makes it abundantly clear throughout the Gospels that we are to love our neighbor and shows us how to help our neighbor through the parable of the Good Samaritan (Luke 10:25–37). In *On Helping One's Neighbor: Severe Poverty and the Religious Ethics of Obligation*, Bharat Ranganathan retrieves this message through the lens of extreme poverty. The author argues that severe poverty is not merely an economic or social problem, but a moral failing which demands ethical reflection and action. Through Catholic ethics and moral philosophy, he shows the potential for Christian ethics to inform and enhance secular approaches to poverty alleviation. Ranganathan advocates for a more comprehensive understanding of ethical obligations toward the poor by transforming ethical principles into concrete actions and policies. The text encourages readers to reflect on their own moral responsibilities and the broader societal obligations to support those in need.

Ranganathan seeks to integrate religious and secular ethical perspectives to motivate individuals, communities, and policymakers to take concrete steps towards reducing poverty. The text is organized systematically to build the argument and explore various facets of the topic. The first chapter discusses religious ethics and obligations to others. In chapter 2, he broadens his arguments to include various political philosophies, with particularly helpful theories of poverty from Peter Singer and Amartya Sen. The third chapter refines these theories as they relate to institutional obligations toward the poor. It becomes more personal in chapter 4 where he argues that the rich have more obligations to the poor than simply to donate to charity; rather, the rich must actively work to simplify their own lives and work to change the unjust structures that contribute to poverty (166). In the final chapter, Ranganathan analyzes the consequences of morality and offers sensible methods for the rich to implement their obligations to the poor. The analysis and practical solutions serve as a motivational framework, encouraging readers to turn ethical principles into action.

Readers of this journal will appreciate Ranganathan's multidimensional approach to ethical obligations regarding justice, human rights, and human dignity. He reinvigorates religious moral teaching with analysis that bridges the gap between Christian moral teaching and the challenges of universal modern ethics. His well-developed argument shows that while specific religious teachings have unique approaches to moral obligations, common ethical imperatives can unite diverse groups in the fight against poverty through interfaith cooperation. Ranganathan emphasizes the practical implications of ethical obligations, encouraging readers to act. Each case study includes careful analysis before offering solutions for real and practical applications. While many affluent persons may readily accept an obligation to provide charity to the poor, there is the potential for controversy in the author's advocacy for simplifying their life. Nevertheless, the text makes a compelling argument based on biblical and theological teaching. These implications provide concrete evidence of how moral theology can impact lives and improve conditions for the poor.

On Helping One's Neighbor offers several notable contributions to moral theology. Ranganathan's book enriches the ethical discourse on poverty by incorporating diverse perspectives and thorough ethical analysis. By addressing severe poverty as a global ethical issue, the author contributes to the broader discourse on global justice. He emphasizes the interconnectedness of global communities and the shared responsibility to address systemic injustices that spread poverty. Ranganathan underscores the role of compassion and empathy in ethical responses to poverty. By advocating for an empathetic approach, the book highlights the importance of understanding and addressing the lived experiences of those suffering from poverty. Moreover, the author's analysis has great potential to stimulate ethical reflection and dialogue. Ranganathan goes beyond individual ethical obligations to consider structural and systemic factors that contribute to severe poverty. This holistic perspective is crucial for understanding the root causes of poverty and developing comprehensive solutions.

Bharat Ranganathan's book successfully integrates religious and secular ethical perspectives, creating a rich, multidisciplinary dialogue. Nevertheless, this attempt to harmonize diverse academic traditions risks oversimplification or a loss of nuance. Some readers may feel that the treatment of certain theological or philosophical theories lacks depth or fails to fully capture their complexities. Nevertheless, the author's thorough analysis should appeal to scholars and others with a deep interest in ethics and religious studies.

This book offers a deep and nuanced understanding of moral obligations towards poverty alleviation with a comprehensive ethical analysis of religious and secular perspectives. This interdisciplinary approach enriches the theological and philosophical study of practical ethics, making it relevant to scholars, practitioners, and policymakers. While the text is structured and priced to be most suitable for a classroom setting, the author's message should be conveyed through the work of other moral theologians in publications that will reach a wider audience. A key strength of the book is its focus on turning ethical principles into practical actions.

NGOC NGUYEN
Marquette University

Deep Inculturation: Global Voices on Christian Faith and Indigenous Genius. Edited by Antonio D. Sison. Maryknoll, NY: Orbis Books, 2024. xxviii + 228 pages. $45.00.

Much of the existing scholarship on inculturation tends to examine the interaction between Western Christianity and local culture as a form of compromise or conflict. In this provocative collection of essays, Antonio Sison offers a challenging and innovative perspective of inculturation as an evolving concept. As he mentions in the introduction, the book intends to renew the discussion of inculturation with consideration of "contextual, inductive, creative, and dialogical approaches" (xvi). The authors emphasize a path of interdisciplinary engagement to unite varied perspectives in creative interaction. While remaining consistent in understanding the introduction of religious practice into new cultures as a mutual relationship that leads to a transformative experience for everyone involved, this collection helps advance the understanding and practice of inculturation.

This two-part volume first addresses the theme of "Ritual and Performance" and concludes with four chapters on "Method and the Lessons of History." Sison's intention is that the collection of essays represents a blend of individual perspectives that offer a harmonious and renewed perspective on inculturation through a "reasoned, appreciative valuation of local culture" (xxvi). *Deep Inculturation* succeeds by presenting seven contributors who offer a diverse interpretation of inculturation through Asian, African, Latin American, and indigenous Australian encounters with European Catholic influences. The individual essays are amalgamated in a collaborative synthesis of liberation theology, Scripture, lived religion, and cultural studies to present a revealing picture of global inculturation.

The most significant contribution to moral theology in this text is the ethical connection of liberation with culture, especially through the perspective of those living on the margins of society. This is most evident in the first chapter, "A Liturgy That Heals," by Christopher Tirres. Here, the author focuses on the implicit ethical dimensions of ritual in a Good Friday liturgy among Mexican American congregants in San Antonio, Texas. This essay shows how the "aesthetics of the moral imagination" (10) allow ritual practices to structure and shape the participants' outlook. Tirres understands morality not in terms of an eternal "moral law" or a "system" of rules for living, but as a deliberation to manage a real-life situation of instability that leads to some form of judgment (14). The ethical implications between liberation and inculturation are refined through the perspectives presented in the subsequent chapters.

While the individual chapters offer valuable and exclusive perspectives on the relationships between culture and religious practices, a hidden gem at the beginning of the text is the foreword by Peter Phan. "Inculturation Revisited" allows Phan to reflect autobiographically on his thoughts about inculturation, his methodology, and what he views as the challenges and how to meet them. This contribution provides necessary context on the study of inculturation for the unique case studies examined in this collection. Phan offers direction in terms of the four rules of inculturation: it must be "contextual," "inductive," "creative," and "dialogical" (viii), and cautions that the challenge for the near future will not be a "lack of initiatives for inculturation at the grassroots level but the Roman

Curia's obsession with hierarchical control and fear of 'heterodox' innovations" (x).

One notable lacuna in this volume on inculturation is the surprising lack of analysis related to Mary, the mother of Jesus. The countless examples of Mary embodying Phan's principles of inculturation are evident in her many apparitions throughout the world. Several authors mention Mary's presence or images in their depictions of rituals, struggles, or devotions, yet there is no substantive analysis of the meaning or importance of inculturation in these Marian encounters. While Sison's comparison of Mary and the Buddhist mother goddess offers a glimpse of this possibility (139), the analysis unfortunately falls short as he moves on to other topics. Likewise, Tirres makes a footnote of inculturation in Marian devotion, yet Mary remains absent from the inculturation discourse throughout the text.

The profound and thoughtful interdisciplinary approach of *Deep Inculturation* offers a vital contribution to the continued evolution of relationships between religious practice and culture. This text, although decidedly Catholic in its approach, should be read by anyone interested in studying the ethical implications and development of relationships between global Christianity and local cultures. To be sure, the authors are not content simply to address the principle of inculturation. Rather, they effectively deconstruct sociological assumptions that have led to continued Eurocentric interpretations of Catholic teaching and its implications throughout the world.

JOE EVANS
Villanova University

Catholic Social Teaching in Practice: Exploring Practical Wisdom and the Virtues. By Andrew M. Yuengert. Cambridge: Cambridge University Press, 2023. xvii + 334 pages. $110.00.

The role of virtues in ethical behavior has always been a central theme in Catholic moral theology. Yuengert's book offers a fresh perspective through its comprehensive exploration of practical wisdom, drawing from the neo-Aristotelian tradition, including the works of Aristotle, Aquinas, and their modern interpreters, within the framework of Catholic social teaching (CST). This enriches CST scholarship, which I have traditionally viewed as deontological due to its focus on principles and human rights. By discussing practical wisdom both as a theoretical object and a virtue in action across CST documents, Yuengert fills a significant lacuna in CST literature: the insufficient attention given to virtues, due partly to the influence of technocratic science and the division of moral theology from social ethics (14).

The book is divided into nine chapters, each highlighting the often-overlooked implications for CST when it is studied through the lens of practical wisdom. Yuengert argues that ethical principles alone are insufficient for dealing with contingencies within ourselves and in the circumstances of our choices (49). He advocates for a perspective that combines Christian faith with practical personalism to guide economic decision-making and social action. I found his examination of the essential role of the laity in social reform and the dialogue between CST and economics particularly illuminating. The author's academic credentials and expertise, as evidenced by the book's extensive and meticulous annotations, lend credibility to the arguments regarding how "the economic account of human nature is mutilated by the absence of virtues . . . by which humans decide how to act and order their lives" (221). He also addresses the political tensions between ecclesiastical authorities and laypeople by situating this within the Thomistic analysis of human acts in order to demonstrate "how people of goodwill might disagree, and . . . the many ways in which we may fail to realize human flourishing through our actions" (257).

While intellectually rigorous, the book explains complex concepts with clarity in a systematic and logical manner, which makes it suitable for classroom use. It can be integrated into course syllabi on virtue ethics, moral theology, or Catholic studies, and is particularly appropriate for upper-level undergraduate and graduate courses. Its careful examination of intricate ideas and original contribution to the subject make it a valuable teaching resource.

Beyond its relevance to Catholicism, Yuengert's interdisciplinary treatment—drawing from philosophy, theology, and economics—enriches the global discourse on virtue ethics by demonstrating its applicability across diverse academic fields. One criticism often leveled against CST as a discipline is its perceived lack of engagement with other religions or intercultural dialogue. Yuengert's approach can meet this challenge. His exploration of cultivating virtue and discerning morally right actions in specific contexts provides universal insights into ethical judgement that resonate with virtue ethicists worldwide, as virtues can be understood from a non-religious point of view. While Western virtue ethics has its roots in ancient Greek culture, similar approaches are also present in Eastern traditions (e.g., Confucianism). Scholars have used virtue ethics as an interpretive framework to articulate the ethical dimensions of African, Islamic, and Filipino philosophies. Yuengert demonstrates how virtue ethics remains relevant today, transcending cultural and religious boundaries. For example, justice—a foundational principle in many ethical traditions—guides individuals and societies toward fairness, equality, and the promotion of the common good (305). In addition, virtue ethics links morality with human flourishing, motivating everyone to lead a moral life, regardless of their religious affiliation or lack thereof.

However, I found that some sections of the book were too abstract and theoretical, potentially challenging readers who lack a strong background in philosophy or theology. Critics might also argue that Yuengert's focus on individual decision-making and personal agency could downplay the significance of addressing power asymmetry and structural injustices embedded in societal institutions. Some readers might desire more direct engagement with contemporary ethical problems and how CST responds to them, such as those concerning bioethics, technology, or emerging social organizations in the digital age.

These critiques are not shortcomings of the book but areas where readers with different academic interests might seek further elaboration. Yuengert's work remains a valuable asset in understanding the connections between CST and social sciences, as well as the limitations of the macro-focused interpretation of CST that emphasizes structural and systemic changes at the expense of individual character formation. The book is particularly relevant for Catholics who seek insight and guidance in applying CST in real-world contexts. By tackling how CST connects with the virtue ethics tradition and how it can be taught practically, this book serves as an excellent resource for theology students and educators in Catholic institutions. Christian faith leaders will find the strategies in the book useful for concretizing CST in their advocacy or pastoral work. Most of all, ethicists will appreciate Yuengert's deep engagement with theological and philosophical ideas.

FERDINAND TABLAN
Seattle University

www.ingramcontent.com/pod-product-compliance
Lightning Source LLC
Chambersburg PA
CBHW070916160426

43193CB00011B/1480